W9-BYC-298

Improve Your Prayer Life

Improve Your Prayer Life

By
Archie Parrish

SERVE INTERNATIONAL • ATLANTA, GEORGIA

Improve Your Prayer Life

Copyright © 2000 by Archie Parrish
Published by Serve International, Inc.
4646 North Shallowford Rd., Suite 200
Atlanta, GA 30338

All rights reserved. No part of this publication may be reproduced, stored in a retrieval system or transmitted in any form by any means, electronic, mechanical, photocopy, recording or otherwise, without the prior permission of the publisher, except as provided by USA copyright law.
All Scripture quotations unless otherwise noted are from *The New King James Version*, copyright © 1984 by Thomas Nelson, Inc. All rights reserved. Used by permission.
Scripture marked NIV taken from the HOLY BIBLE: NEW INTERNATIONAL VERSION ®. Copyright © 1973, 1978, 1984 by International Bible Society. Used by permission of Zondervan Publishing House. All rights reserved.
The "NIV" and "New International Version" trademarks are registered in the United States Patent and Trademark Office by International Bible Society. Use of either trademark requires the permission of International Bible Society.

First printing, 2000
Printed in the United States of America
ISBN 1-930976-00-3

Table of Contents

Before You Begin

Improve Your Prayer Life is more than just another book on prayer—it is a training manual and, when properly used, it will transform your instinctive, reactive prayer into biblical, proactive, kingdom-focused prayer. The material included here is designed to be used for stage one of *The Kingdom Campaign,*[1] a movement aimed at building a super-critical mass composed of 120 kingdom intercessors in 120 local churches in 120 metro areas in North America. The objective of *The Kingdom Campaign* is twofold: to equip believers to develop the daily discipline of kingdom-focused prayer, and to encourage them to multiply after their kind, that is, to train others to do the same.

I challenge you to invest the next ninety (90) days in extraordinary kingdom-focused prayer. Extraordinary prayer goes beyond the usual public prayer of the worship service or Bible study. It goes further than the usual grace at meals. Kingdom-focused prayer is not mere instinctive, self-serving, man-centered, sentimental, timid, solo, passive resignation to fate. Kingdom-focused prayer is Spirit-enabled, God-centered,

---

[1] If you have not read the free sixteen-page booklet, *The Kingdom Campaign* (available from Serve International, 4646 N. Shallowford Rd., Suite 200, Atlanta, GA 30338), please do so now. It describes the best process for learning the material in this book and implementing a supercritical mass of kingdom-focused prayer in your local church. It will explain the foundations upon which *Improve Your Prayer Life* is built, and will also show the role of the other books in the Kingdom Campaign series: *Intercede For and With Your Family; Invigorate Your Church; Impact Your World;* and *Ignite Your Leadership* (Leader's Guide for the series).

fervent, persistent, kingdom-serving, concerted, active cooperation with the will of the Father.

No matter how young you are it is not too soon to become a person of prayer! Samuel was but a boy when he prayed, *"Speak LORD, for Your servant hears."*[2] Then the Lord said, *"Behold, I will do something in Israel at which both ears of everyone who hears it will tingle."*[3]

Kingdom-focused prayer is Spirit-enabled, God-centered, fervent, persistent, kingdom-serving, concerted, active cooperation with the will of the Father.

No matter how old you are, it is not too late to become a person of prayer! Caleb, at 85, was still ready to take on the difficult task of scaling the mountains and driving out the Philistines.[4] No matter what your past frustrations may have been, no matter what your past failings, becoming a kingdom intercessor can make you more effective. The rest of your life can be the best of your life!

As you learn to pray with a kingdom focus, remember that Christ is the King of the kingdom. He is seated at the Father's *"right hand in the heavenly places."*[5] There He always lives to make *"intercession for us."*[6] As believers, God has *"raised us up together, and made us sit together in the heavenly places in Christ Jesus."*[7] Positionally, you are now close enough to

---

[2] 1 Samuel 3:9

[3] 1 Samuel 3:11

[4] Joshua 14:6-12

[5] Ephesians 1:20

[6] Romans 8:34. Also see Hebrews 7:25.

[7] Ephesians 2:6

8

Christ to hear His intercession. Picture yourself listening to the Lord Jesus and seek to echo to the Father the intercession of the Son.

What are you to echo? Pray for His Church *"which He purchased with His own blood."*[8] Intercede for its shepherds.[9] Paul tells us *"first of all, that requests, prayers, intercession and thanksgiving be made for everyone."*[10] Pray for your fellow church members. For your prayers to be most effective, you must embrace others. Your local church is one of the most significant factors in shaping your prayer life.

As believers, God has *"raised us up together, and made us sit together in the heavenly places in Christ Jesus."* Positionally, you are now close enough to Christ to hear His intercession. Picture yourself listening to the Lord Jesus and seek to echo to the Father the intercession of the Son.

In order to use the material provided to train yourself to improve your prayer life, it will be necessary to plan time to work through the material in this book, as well as to plan time to pray. Be sure to read the introductory remarks of the *Discussion Guide* (pages 107 through 118) before you begin reading the text on page 11! You will find directions there for working through the text and for developing the daily discipline of kingdom-focused prayer. It will also tell you how the accompanying text, *A Simple Way to Pray,* is to be used.

---

[8] Acts 20:28

[9] See 1 Timothy 3:1-7.

[10] 1 Timothy 2:1-5 NIV

I hope you will take my challenge for the next ninety days—to prayerfully work through the material in this book as a member of a four-person fireteam. If you do, I know you will experience increased fruitfulness and joy!

No matter how young you are it is not too soon to become a person of prayer. No matter how old you are, it is not too late to become a person of prayer. The rest of your life can be the best of your life!

•••••

We Cannot Know
What Prayer is for Until ...

I need to start by confessing a major sin that for more than thirty years diminished God's power in my life and ministry. From conversations with many other Christian leaders, lay and ordained, I estimate that at least eight out of ten are presently struggling with this same sin. Many who commit it are unaware that they are doing so. They may be conscious of the symptoms—lack of joy, lack of power, lack of the fruit of the Spirit in their lives, and lack of fruitfulness in winning the lost—but they most likely have not connected these symptoms to the source of the problem—*being a prayerless leader of prayerless people.* OUCH

In Samuel's farewell speech to the people of Israel, we see the biblical mandate:

> *Do not fear. You have done all this wickedness; yet do not turn aside from following the LORD, but serve the LORD with all your heart. And do not turn aside; for then you would go after empty things which cannot profit or deliver, for they are nothing. For the LORD will not forsake His people, for His great name's sake, because it has pleased the LORD to make you His people. Moreover, as for me, far be it from me that I should sin against the LORD in ceasing to pray for you; but I will teach you the good and the right way. Only fear the LORD, and serve Him in truth with all your heart; for consider what great things He has done for you. But if you still do wickedly, you shall be swept away, both you and your king.*[11]

---

[11] 1 Samuel 12:20-25

Through more than thirty years of training and ministry, I prayed. But I never became a man of prayer. The Apostles said, *"We will give ourselves continually to prayer and the ministry of the word."*[12] Only when the ministry of the word is united with prayer does God release the fullness of His gracious power.

When the Berlin Wall fell, I was asked to work with new believers in Russia. They needed basic discipleship material for the great numbers of new converts. I asked my friend, Ravi Zacharias, to read the material I developed and he challenged me to search more deeply into what prayer really is. He suggested that I read C. S. Lewis' *Letters to Malcolm*. This opened a vista so grand that six years later, I am still marveling in new discoveries.

> **Only when the ministry of the word is united with prayer does God release the fullness of His gracious power.**

When I started my quest for a deeper understanding of prayer, I collected in my word processor every passage of Scripture dealing with prayer from Genesis to Revelation. At this same time, I began reading everything I could find on the subject of prayer. It did not take long to realize that much of the modern writing on this subject is filled with sentimental, self-centered drivel. But as I searched, I found writings by men of prayer whom God used to change the course of history—Luther, Calvin, Knox, Edwards, Forsyth, Sibbs, Gurnall, Bounds, Lewis, and many others.

Prayer is now the central focus for *all* of my study and ministry. For six years, I have had one basic goal for my life— to develop such an intimate relationship with God through prayer that when I die I will change location (from earth to heaven), but my primary companion will still be the Lord.

---

[12] Acts 6:4

P. T. Forsyth begins his classic volume, *The Soul of Prayer,* with these words, "It is a difficult and even formidable thing to write on prayer, one fears to touch the ark. Perhaps no one ought to undertake it unless he has spent more toil in the practice of prayer than on its principle. But perhaps also the effort to look into its principle may be graciously regarded by Him who ever lives to make intercession as itself a prayer to know better how to pray."[13] This book is my prayer to know better how to pray.

I have struggled with presuming to write on a subject about which I still have much to learn. The more I know about prayer the more aware I am that there is so much more that I don't know. For six years now I have collected my meditations on Scripture and the insights of prayer warriors from the past. I have led more than sixty schools of prayer. It is the need for manuals for those who participate in these events that finally convinced me to write this book. The Lord willing, this volume will be the first in a series facilitating *The Kingdom Campaign,* a movement aimed at building a super-critical mass composed of 120 kingdom intercessors in 120 local churches in 120 metro areas in North America.

George Barna studied churches that turned around after statistical plateau or decline. Of these churches, he observed, "Prayer must permeate the ministry. A healthy church is a praying church as determined by the number of people who pray, the frequency with which they pray, the intensity with which they pray, and the joy they experience from their prayers. If God is really believed to be the power source and prayer is seen as our means of communication with Him, a church's faith can be determined by the condition of its prayer life."[14]

---

[13] P.T. Forsyth, *The Soul of Prayer,* Eerdmans Publishing, Grand Rapids, MI, 1916, p. 11.

[14] George Barna, *Turn-Around Churches*, Regal Books, Ventura, CA, 1993, p. 105.

How do we become people of prayer? Prayer cannot be learned by merely reading or talking about it. Discussing prayer is not praying. To learn to pray, we must pray. John Piper has said, "We cannot know what prayer is for until we know that life is war."[15] This book explains why life is war, and what prayer is for. It uses an approach to prayer that is militant and sometimes even military, but it is not limited to use by those who have experienced military service or combat. The unique contribution of this book is the basic training it provides to become a prayer warrior, i.e., a kingdom intercessor, effectively functioning in a spiritual army and encouraging others to do likewise.

> **Prayer cannot be learned by merely reading or talking about it. To learn to pray, we must pray.**

God has built into all creation the principle that living things *"multiply after their kind."*[16] Paul indicates multiplication is important in the realm of the spiritual also. To Timothy he said, *"The things that you have heard from me among many witnesses, commit these to faithful men who will be able to teach others also."*[17] The primary purpose of this book is *not* to develop solo, super-saints; it is to build fireteams composed of committed believers who encourage each other to fifteen minutes of daily kingdom-focused prayer, and to multiply after their kind by starting additional fireteams that do the same.

Before proceeding to study kingdom-focused prayer, let's take a survey—to help us see the present reality of our prayer life. On each item, mark which answer best describes your belief or present practice. The results will most likely be quite revealing!

---

[15] John Piper, *Let the Nations Be Glad! The Supremacy of God in Missions,* Baker Books, Grand Rapids, MI, 1993, p. 41.

[16] See Genesis 1:11-12, 21, 24-25.

[17] 2 Timothy 2:2

Prayer Survey

1. It is important to thank God for His faithfulness and grace.

        1   2   3   4   5
    Strongly disagree   Strongly agree

2. I pause and thank God for my food.

    __Seldom __Occasionally __Weekly __Daily __At each meal

3. Christians should pray for their local church leaders.

        1   2   3   4   5
    Strongly disagree   Strongly agree

4. I pray for the leaders of my local church.

    __Seldom __Occasionally __Weekly __Daily __At each meal

5. Christians should pray for their pastors.

        1   2   3   4   5
    Strongly disagree   Strongly agree

6. I pray for my pastor(s) by name.

    __Seldom __Occasionally __Weekly __Daily __At each meal

7. Christians should pray for the salvation of non-Christians.

        1   2   3   4   5
    Strongly disagree   Strongly agree

8. I pray for the salvation of specific non-Christians in my sphere of influence.

    __Never __Seldom __Occasionally __Weekly __Daily

9. Christians should pray for the workers needed for local church ministry.

        1   2   3   4   5
    Strongly disagree   Strongly agree

10. I pray for the Lord to send the workers needed for my local church's ministry.

    __Never __Seldom __Occasionally __Weekly __Daily

11. Effective prayer is essential for healthy Christian living.

     1   2   3   4   5

Strongly disagree   Strongly agree

12. My prayer life is as effective as it should be.

     1   2   3   4   5

Strongly disagree   Strongly agree

13. In the past 30 days, specific answers to my prayers, to which I can point, total …

__0 __1-5 __6-15 __15-30 __31+

14. Christians should invest time in prayer.

     1   2   3   4   5

Strongly disagree   Strongly agree

15. I invest as much time in prayer as I should.

     1   2   3   4   5

Strongly disagree   Strongly agree

16. Each day, the number of minutes I pray is …

__15 or less __15-30 __30-45 __45-60 __60+

17. Married couples should pray together.

     1   2   3   4   5

Strongly disagree   Strongly agree

18. Other than grace at meals, I pray with my spouse …

__Never __Seldom __Occasionally __Weekly __Daily

19. Parents should pray with their young children.

     1   2   3   4   5

Strongly disagree   Strongly agree

20. Other than grace at meals, I pray with my children …

__Never __Seldom __Occasionally __Weekly __Daily

My Observations

And you shall know the truth, and the truth shall make you free.[18]

In examining life, or any aspect of it, it is most important to determine what reality is. What is the reality of your prayer life? The survey you have just completed provides a snapshot of your present situation; it is a snapshot of your prayer beliefs and practice.

Most people who take this survey find there is a gap between what they say they believe and how they behave. For example:

- Many people believe it is important to thank God for His faithfulness and grace, but do not consistently pause to thank God for the food they eat, especially when they "eat out."
- Many people think they should pray for their church leaders but do it only occasionally.
- Most believe they should pray for the salvation of specific non-Christians in their sphere of influence but less than 10% do this on a daily basis.
- Most believe they should ask the Lord of the Harvest to send workers to their church, but very few give this high priority in their prayers.
- All who have taken this survey believe effective prayer is essential for healthy Christian living, but none say their prayer life is as effective as it should be.
- All believe Christians should invest time in prayer, but most invest less than fifteen minutes daily in prayer.
- Almost all married couples believe they should pray together, but for most this is only an occasional practice.
- Almost all parents believe they should pray with and for their children, but this also is only an occasional practice.
- Most husbands pray with their children more than they do with their wives.

---

[18] John 8:32

17

The difference between what we say we believe and how we behave has been called the "sanctification gap." One of the main purposes of this book is to help us close this gap in regard to our prayer life. When our beliefs and our behavior properly correspond, we have a sense of wholeness and power. Then we understand what Jesus meant when He said, *"You shall know the truth, and the truth shall make you free."* [19]

The difference between what we say we believe and how we behave has been called the "sanctification gap." One of the main purposes of this book is to help us close this gap in regard to our prayer life.

•••••

---

[19] John 8:32

Life is War

"Peace has broken out in less than eight percent of all history! Out of 3,453 years of recorded history, only 268 years are without war. War is a constant on the stage of human history."[20]

God ordained governments to maintain order within nations. His word declares, *"Therefore whoever resists the authority resists the ordinance of God, and those who resist will bring judgment on themselves. For rulers are not a terror to good works, but to evil. Do you want to be unafraid of the authority? Do what is good, and you will have praise from the same. For he is God's minister to you for good. But if you do evil, be afraid; for he does not bear the sword in vain; for he is God's minister, an avenger to execute wrath on him who practices evil."*[21] Governments maintain police to deal with lawbreakers within the nation, and they maintain military forces to protect their nation from enemies without.

When governments allow inequity to go unchecked, within or without, over a period of time, God's longsuffering runs out and judgment falls. Sometimes God judges directly (e.g., the destruction of Sodom and Gomorrah, and the great flood in the

---

[20] Will and Ariel Durant, *The Lessons of History,* Simon and Schuster, New York, 1968, p. 81. The Durants, in 1968, said that there were 3,421 years of recorded history. I write in 2000, 32 years later. There has not been one year in the last 32 without war. Therefore, the total now is 3,453.

[21] Romans 13:2-4

days of Noah). Other times God uses one nation to carry out His judgment on another nation (e.g., the Israelites' defeat of the Amorites[22]).

Military war is "a state of hostilities that exists between or among nations, characterized by the use of military force. The essence of war is a violent clash between two hostile, independent and irreconcilable wills, each trying to impose itself on the other. In this environment, friction abounds."[23] Thus military war deals in death and destruction.

The Apostle James asks, *"Where do wars and fights come from among you?"* And he answers his own question, *"Do they not come from your desires for pleasure that war in your members? You lust and do not have. You murder and covet and cannot obtain. You fight and war. Yet you do not have because you do not ask. You ask and do not receive, because you ask amiss, that you may spend it on your pleasures."*[24] War, fights, lust, and murder come from not praying, or from praying for one's selfish pleasure.

Three Assumptions

In order to learn more about the essence of war, let's first consider three basic assumptions. First, wars bring out the worst and the best in people, but they never leave people the same as they were before the war. In his helpful book, *The Fight,* John White emphasizes war's positive results:

> Wars produce the noblest and best in a man: unnatural courage, unbelievable self-sacrifice, devotion, loyalty

---

[22] Numbers 21:21-35

[23] *Warfighting: The United States Marine Corps*, by U. S. Marine Corps Staff, 1989, p. 3.

[24] James 4:1-3

and love, resourcefulness in the face of impossible odds, endurance beyond the limits of human strength. The Holy Spirit uses the image of warfare to convey the nature of Christian living. No image could be more apt. The same courage, the same watchfulness, loyalty, endurance, resourcefulness, strength, skill, knowledge of the enemy, the same undying resolve to fight to the end, come what may, and at whatever cost must characterize Christian living as they do earthly warfare.[25]

Our second assumption is that organized armies, not mobs or individuals, win military battles. One person can start a war, but one person, all by himself, can never win a war.

Wars bring out the worst and the best in people, but they never leave people the same as they were before the war.

Third, military wars are composed of many battles. It is possible to lose battles yet win the war, and it is also possible to win battles yet lose the war. Even after decisive battles that seal the destiny of a nation, there can be bloody battles before the war is over. Historians say that the Allies winning of World War II in Europe was inevitable after they established the beachhead at Normandy. However, battles still raged until Berlin fell.

The same is true about spiritual warfare. The decisive battle in the cosmic conflict between God and the devil was fought on Good Friday, and won by Christ on Easter morning. The destiny of all believers was sealed that day, but until Christ's return, the spiritual war will not be over. Within time and space, spiritual battles will continue to rage. In this book, we

---

[25] John White, *The Fight*, InterVarsity Press, Downers Grove, IL 1976, p. 216.

want to look into spiritual warfare from God's perspective so that we will know better how to exercise ourselves *"toward godliness"*[26] and be equipped as prayer warriors.

Organized armies, not mobs or individuals, win military battles.

To do this, we will first learn some basic principles of military war to give us a framework for study. Then, we will focus on warfare in the Bible, contrasting military war with holy war. Last, we will identify some lessons that will help us win spiritual battles.

Six Aspects of a Military Model

The six aspects of a military model we will consider are: paradigm shift, leaders, soldiers, organization, intelligence and weapons.

Paradigm Shift

A paradigm is "a set of rules and regulations (written or unwritten) that does two things: it establishes or defines boundaries; and it tells you how to behave inside the boundaries in order to be successful."[27] A great paradigm shift is needed from civilian life to military life. Civilians are pretty much able to do what they desire when they desire to do it. The boundaries of military life and how people must function in them will be evident as we proceed.

---

[26] 1 Timothy 4:7

[27] Joel Arthur Barker, *Future Edge,* Wm. Morrow & Co., New York, NY, 1992, p. 32.

Leaders

Every organization must have leaders. William A. Cohen provides an illustration from nature that underscores the necessity of leadership.

There is a strange insect called the processionary caterpillar. This insect bears this unusual name because of its unusual way of navigation. A number of processionary caterpillars will attach themselves front to back in a single line. The leader seeks the mulberry leaf, the main food for the caterpillar. Wherever the leader goes, the other processionary caterpillars are sure to follow, and off they go in this way, one continuous line of five or more caterpillars looking for mulberry leaves.

Several years ago a scientist conducted an experiment by taking a line of processionary caterpillars and forming them into a circle. The leader was attached to the back of the last caterpillar in the line so that now there was no leader; all were follower caterpillars. In the center of the circle of caterpillars, he placed a bowl of mulberry leaves. The scientist wanted to know how long they would maintain the circle with no leader and no objective.

The result of the experiment surprised him. The caterpillars continued in the circle until they were so weak they couldn't reach the mulberry leaves. Though food was only inches away, they continued to follow the caterpillar in front, going forward with no objective at all.[28]

Leadership involves more than just being at the head of the line. Leaders must be brilliant, bold, and brave. General

---

[28] William A. Cohen, *The Art of the Leader*, Prentice Hall, New Jersey, 1990, pp. 32-33.

Thomas "Stonewall" Jackson admonished, "Do not take counsel of your fears."[29] Courage is at the heart of a warrior's core values. Courage that is required for combat is not the absence of fear; it is the ability to overcome fear. James Woulfe said courage "is composed of mental, moral, and physical strengths that are ingrained in all Marines to carry them through the challenges of combat and allow them to master their fears. Courage will help them do what is right by adhering to a high standard of personal conduct, leading by example, and making tough decisions under stress and pressure."[30]

Soldiers

Soldiers must also be able-bodied, fit, courageous, and mature. They must be able to do what needs to be done even when it may result in being wounded or death. Good soldiers are not individuals, but team members. Discipline is required to be a good soldier; that is described in more detail below. In his classic, *On War*, Carl von Clausewitz, emphasizes the principle of "superiority of numbers."[31] Usually the army with the greater number of soldiers wins the battle.

Organization

Armies must have at least fundamental organization, including the chain of command and discipline. "These factors make all the difference between an army, however primitive, and

---

[29] *Warfighting: The United States Marine Corps*, by U. S. Marine Corps Staff, 1989, p. 13.

[30] James B. Woulfe, *Into the Crucible, Making Marines for the 21st Century,* Presidio Press, Navato, CA, 1998, pgs. 17, 33.

[31] Carl von Clausewitz, *On War,* "Relative Strength," Book 3, Chapter Three, pages 282-284; "Superiority of Numbers," Book 3, Chapter Eight, pages 194-197; Edited and translated by Michael Howard and Peter Paret, Princeton University Press, Princeton, NJ, 1976.

unsophisticated, and armed rabble."[32]   For centuries, the military has utilized the chain of command to insure maximum impact on the enemy while sustaining minimum loss of life among its own troops. This chain of command runs from the Commander-in-Chief at the top down to the fireteams in the field.   Tom Clancy speaks of the value of the chain of command in the modern U. S. Marine Corps:

> Marines have a sense of their personal identity and position in the world. Ask any marine and he or she will be able to trace the chain of command all the way from himself or herself right up to the President of the United States. This is not simply a trick, like dogs walking on their hind legs. It is an indication that every marine is confident of his or her place in the world. And that shows in confident behavior. More important, Marines learn that they are trusted to make good decisions, follow orders and accomplish tasks in the best way available. If you have worked for a big corporation with numbing layers of middle management over your head and no sense of personal empowerment, you can appreciate the refreshing clarity that Marines feel about their individual positions and missions.[33]

Without discipline, the military chain of command is useless. It is discipline that enables a soldier in combat to do what is necessary in spite of risk to life and limb. Woulfe explains, "This discipline grows out of the spirit of determination and dedication within members of a force of arms that leads to professionalism and mastery of the art of war. It leads to the highest level of dedication for the unit and self and it is the

---

[32] Chaim Herzog and Mordechai Gichon, *Battles of the Bible*, Greenhill Books, London revised edition, 1997, p. 38.

[33] Tom Clancy, *Marine, A Guided Tour of a Marine Expeditionary Unit,* Berkley Books, New York, 1993, p. 45.

ingredient that enables twenty-four-hour-a-day devotion to Corps and country."[34]

Woulfe continues, "Discipline must be framed in positive, desirable terms, not be imposed from the outside but embraced as a trait and habit, a self-discipline that comes from a deep internal need to excel. Self-discipline is doing the right thing even when it is not the natural thing to do. It is based on pride in the profession of arms, on meticulous attention to details, and on mutual respect and confidence. Self-discipline must be so ingrained that it is stronger than the excitement of battle or the fear of death."[35]

General George Patton said, "All human beings have an innate resistance to obedience. Discipline removes this resistance, and, by constant repetition, makes obedience habitual and subconscious. Where would an undisciplined football team get? Only when players react subconsciously to the signals can the team win. The players must act reflexively because the split second required for thought would give the enemy the jump. Battle is much more exigent than football. No *sane* man is unafraid in battle, but discipline produces in him a vicarious courage, which with his manhood, makes for victory."[36]

Intelligence

Armies are most effective when they know the enemy well. From the first days of tribal wars, military intelligence activities have been very important. The great captains of history have each in his time devoted much of their time to outguessing and outwitting their foes by acquiring as accurate a

---

[34] James B. Woulfe, *Into the Crucible, Making Marines for the 21st Century,* Presidio Press, Navato, CA, 1998, p. 41.

[35] Ibid., p. 74.

[36] Alan Axelrod, *Patton on Leadership, Strategic Lessons for Corporate Warfare,* Prentice Hall, Paramus, N.J., 1999, p. 175-176, 207

picture as possible of their foes' intentions, strength, deployment, terrain, and capabilities. Capabilities of nations in war and peace are based on their natural and industrial resources, their political stability and demography, the character and stamina of their populations, their armed forces, their scientific endeavor, their topography and infrastructure.

Weapons

Armies also need adequate offensive and defensive weapons. Since life and victory usually depend on weapons, keeping them in good working order must always come first. In combat, the soldier's weapon is more important than his food. In modern war, sophisticated high-tech long-range weapons are essential, but ultimately on the human level, the keeping of the peace comes back to the soldier and his rifle.

To summarize, "the essence of war is a violent clash between two hostile, independent and irreconcilable wills, each trying to impose itself on the other."[37] We have also seen six important aspects of a military model: a great paradigm shift; leadership; organization; disciplined, brave soldiers; intelligence; and superior weapons. However, as B. H. Liddell Hart says, "In war, the chief incalculable is the human will."[38] General A. A. Vandergrif reinforces this thought, "Positions are seldom lost because they have been destroyed, but almost invariably because the leader has decided in his own mind that the position cannot be held."[39] The Marine training manual, *Warfighting,* is correct, "Only through experience can we come to appreciate the force of will necessary to overcome friction

---

[37] *Warfighting: The United States Marine Corps*, by U. S. Marine Corps Staff, 1989, p. 3.

[38] Quoted in *Warfighting: The United States Marine Corps*, by U. S. Marine Corps Staff, 1989, p. 1.

[39] Ibid., p. 10.

and develop a realistic appreciation for what is possible in war and what is not."[40]

Wars are composed of many battles. It is possible to lose battles yet win the war, and it is also possible to win battles yet lose the war.

My Experience

When I was fifteen, I saw *The Sands of Iwo Jima,* a film in which John Wayne played the role of Sergeant Striker, a drill instructor in the Marines. World War II had concluded just three years before and the fire of patriotism was still burning bright. I decided to join the Marines. So I went to the recruiting office in Oklahoma City and swaggered up to the sergeant's desk. He stood up and I felt like I was face-to-face with Sergeant Striker himself. He had hash marks from his wrist to his elbow, indicating more than twenty years of active service as a leatherneck. On his chest were rows of combat ribbons. I flippantly said, "Sarge, what do you have to offer?"

"Six years of hell," he barked back, "but you're not man enough to take it. Get out of here and don't waste my time!"

"Well," I thought to myself, "if this is how you feel, I will join the Navy." And that's just what I did. The chief boson's mate in the Navy recruiting office had also enlisted when he was fifteen. He showed me how to use the record page in a family Bible as a birth certificate and he helped me with the tests.

After I passed all the exams, the chief told me that the best job in the Navy was being a medical corpsman. "They always

---

[40] *Warfighting: The United States Marine Corps,* by U. S. Marine Corps Staff, 1989, p. 5.

sleep between clean sheets, have good food and lots of free time," said the chief. This sounded good to me, so I requested hospital corps training—and got it.

My first assignment was the Balboa Naval Hospital—night duty on the dependent's ward. All night I attended to expectant mothers in the labor rooms. This was *not* the travel, adventure, and education for which I had joined the Navy! After a few days, I went to the personnel office and pleaded for an assignment that was manlier. The personnel officer asked if I was interested in duty with the Fleet Marine Force. "What's that?" I asked.

"The Marines are part of the Navy, so we provide them with doctors and hospital corpsmen. When you volunteer to serve with the Marines—you also get credit for sea duty without going to sea."

That word "volunteer" should have been a red flag, but I was young, ignorant, and eager for a transfer. Seven months later my orders came. I was assigned to Camp LeJune, NC. During the next two years, there were war games in Newfoundland and Puerto Rico. I learned to strip my carbine, to combat load a field hospital, to climb down cargo nets into landing craft, and "hit the beach." One officer said the goal of our training was to develop men who could march twenty miles in a day carrying a pack that weighed one-hundred pounds and arrive ready to destroy the enemy. It was challenging, but it was just a game. Until Sunday, June 25, 1950!

I was home on leave when I heard the news flash on the radio. The North Korean army had invaded South Korea. The next day, my leave was canceled and I was ordered back to the base. Most of the men of the 2nd Division were sent to Camp Pendleton, California. Reservists by the hundreds swarmed into Pendleton's Quonset huts. Some of the reservists were World War II veterans, but many of them were young men who had enlisted just to get a little spending money. President Truman had attacked the Marines shortly before the Inchon invasion and branded them as "nothing but a police force." In response, many of the Division's vehicles were painted crudely: "Truman's Police" and tanks bore the legend "MP."

General George Patton said, "Compared to war, all other human endeavors pale into insignificance."[41] I found this to be true! On September 15th, the 1st Marine Division invaded Inchon. This was not a John Wayne film. The sixteen-inch guns of the battleship Missouri thundered death and destruction broadsides into the city. Blue Marine and Navy Corsairs fighter planes flew close support for the infantry, strafing and dropping napalm bombs. There were *real* casualties! In the seven days following D-day there were 1148 marine casualties, 145 of them killed; 20 more died of wounds and 5 were missing.[42] It seemed to me that most of them were young reservists. In one day, I helped recover six bodies off a hill— not one was over eighteen years old. Over the next few months, my view of war radically changed.

The Korean War marked the first time the United States went to war without using its full range of weapons. The atomic bombs that staggered the Japanese to surrender in 1945 were denied to the military. Consequently, the Korean War was the first time America fought a war to an unvictorious conclusion. President Truman had put limits on the war that made it impossible to win. The bloody police action in Korea lasted just short of thirty-eight months and cost more than 2,000,000 lives—North Korean soldiers, civilians from both the North and the South, Chinese troops, United Nations military personnel and 52,246 Americans.

---

[41] Quoted in *Warfighting: The United States Marine Corps*, by U. S. Marine Corps Staff, 1989, p. 7.

[42] Burke Davis, *Marine! The Life of Chesty Puller, The Only Marine in History to Win Five Navy Crosses*, Bantam Books, New York, 1964, p. 247.

My combat experience in Korea has influenced everything in my life since then. It has greatly helped me understand spiritual warfare. That is why I frequently refer to the Marines Corps for illustrations in this book. My experience with the Marines in Korea significantly influenced the past forty-seven years of my Christian life and ministry from which this book grows.

So far, we have seen that we must pray because "life is war," and we have been given a framework or model of what is involved in military war. In the next chapter, *War in the Bible*, we will use that framework to consider holy war as it is found in the Scriptures of the Old and New Testaments.

•••••

War in the Bible

Then all this assembly shall know that the LORD does not save with sword and spear; for the battle is the LORD'S, and He will give you into our hands.[43]

"The whole Bible is crowned with a book all sounding with battle cries, the shouts and songs of soldiers, till it ends with that city of peace where they hang the trumpets in the hall and study war no more."[44]

Two modern Israeli military experts recognize the place of warfare in the pages of the Bible. "We have been able to reaffirm that the strategic and tactical lessons of the Bible are as relevant as ever."[45] Thus wrote Chaim Herzog and Mordechi Gichon in their intriguing book, *Battles of the Bible.* Herzog served in the British Army during World War II and then in the Israel Defense Forces, and was thereafter Director of Israeli Military Intelligence, Military Governor of the West Bank, Israel's Ambassador to the United Nations, and President of Israel. Gichon is also an expert in military history, geography and archaeology of Israel in earlier periods; he served in the British Army during World War II, and in the Israeli Defense Forces in a variety of senior intelligence posts.

---

[43] 1 Samuel 17:47

[44] Alexander Whyte, *Bunyan Characters of the Holy War,* Oliphant, Anderson and Ferrier, London, 1902, p 10.

[45] Chaim Herzog and Mordechai Gichon, *Battles of the Bible*, Greenhill Books, London revised edition 1997, p. 24.

He has also held major academic positions at Tel Aviv University.

These two men write from a *mere* military perspective. They overlook the fact that many of the battles recorded in the Old Testament are, in fact, "holy war"—a term used to refer to conflict between the chosen people of God and their enemies.

Holy War in the Old Testament

The first reference in the Bible to the warlike nature of God is found in Exodus. *"Then Moses and the children of Israel sang this song to the LORD, and spoke, saying:*
'I will sing to the LORD,
For He has triumphed gloriously!
The horse and its rider
He has thrown into the sea!
The LORD is my strength and song,
And He has become my salvation;
He is my God, and I will praise Him;
My father's God, and I will exalt Him.
The LORD is a man of war;
The LORD is His name.'" [46]
The objective of holy war in this passage was Israel's conquest and occupation of the Promised Land and the punishment of the wicked Amorites.

We find the parameters for waging this holy war in Deuteronomy 7 and 20. God tells Israel He is now going to give them the land He promised to their fathers. [47] Seven nations *"greater and mightier than"* Israel are named. [48] Israel

---

[46] Exodus 15:1-3

[47] Deuteronomy 7:13

[48] Deuteronomy 7:1

is to *"conquer them and utterly destroy them."*[49] The Lord
reminds Israel of the signs and wonders He performed to gain
their release from Egypt.[50] He promises to drive out the
nations little by little, lest the beasts of the field become too
numerous for them.[51] When they are on the verge of battle, the
priest is to send all the distracted and fainthearted home.[52]
Captains are appointed to lead the people.[53] Israel is to offer
peace to nations that are not among the cursed seven and if
their peace is received, the people will be spared and pay
tribute to Israel.[54] If the peace is not received, every male in
the city is to be destroyed. As an inheritance, the Lord will
give Israel the cities of Hittites, the Amorites, the Canaanites,
the Perizzites, the Hivites, and the Jebusites. In these cities
nothing that breathes is to remain alive.[55]

In studying war in the Old Testament, we see that *Jehovah*
always initiated holy war, never Israel. God did not agree to
grant victory for every circumstance in which Israel found
itself. God expected Israel to prepare for and execute battles
utilizing the aspects of warfare described below; but Israel was
never to trust in her strategy, tactics, intelligence, organization,
weapons, etc. God made this vividly clear to the Israelites
when the *"commander of the army of the LORD"* appeared to
Joshua on the eve of the destruction of Jericho.[56] The episode
recounts an unsolicited appearance of God to Joshua where
God not only commanded Joshua to destroy the city, but also

---

49 Deuteronomy 7:2

50 Deuteronomy 7:18

51 Deuteronomy 7:22

52 Deuteronomy 20:2-9

53 Deuteronomy 20:9

54 Deuteronomy 20:10

55 Deuteronomy 20:16-17

56 Joshua 5:13-15

gave him a detailed battle strategy.[57]   God could have accomplished all this with a single word. But, He chose to use Israel as the means to gain the victory in order to help them trust *Him*, not their strategy, tactics, intelligence or weapons. God also chose to use Israel to show the enemy that the people of Israel were indeed His chosen ones.

Let's see how our framework of six aspects of a military model fits with the scriptural picture of holy war.

Paradigm Shift

As we saw earlier, a paradigm is "a set of rules and regulations (written or unwritten) that does two things: it establishes or defines boundaries; and it tells you how to behave inside the boundaries in order to be successful."[58] A paradigm shift was necessary for Israel's conquest and occupation of the Holy Land.

In Exodus, Moses tells of a new Pharaoh or king over Egypt, one who had not heard of Joseph and the position he had held in Egypt. This king was afraid the Israelites, who were more numerous than the Egyptians, might join Egypt's enemies, fight with them against Egypt, and leave the kingdom. The king decided to set taskmasters over the Israelites, and afflict them with heavy burdens. This made their lives bitter with hard bondage. Perhaps the ultimate agony was the day Pharaoh commanded, *"Every son who is born you shall cast into the river, and every daughter you shall save alive."*[59] It was dangerous to be the son of an Israelite in those days!

---

[57] Joshua 6:2-5

[58] Joel Arthur Barker, *Future Edge,* Wm. Morrow & Co., New York, NY, 1992, p. 32.

[59] Exodus 1:8-22

Working as slave labor hardened the Israelites' bodies, but it broke their wills. Their prayer became a continuous groan in God's ear[60], so He raised up Moses and sent him to tell Pharaoh, *"Thus says the LORD: 'Israel is My son, My firstborn. So I say to you, let My son go that he may serve Me.'"*[61] What followed was a power encounter between Moses and Pharaoh! God visited Egypt with ten plagues and then climaxed the conflict by drowning the Egyptian army in the Red Sea.[62] Yet, in spite of God's extraordinary intervention, the Israelites still thought and acted like slaves. They saw themselves as less than human. They saw themselves as grasshoppers. This self-image limited their ability to behave like *Jehovah's* sons. They were not ready to conquer the Promised Land. They *said* they wanted freedom but when they got it, they were afraid of the responsibilities that went with it.

At the time of the exodus from Egypt, Israel was unarmed rabble. This is clearly seen in the reaction of the masses to the bad report of the ten spies. In spite of witnessing God's power in the ten plagues and the incredible parting of the Red Sea, the masses believed the majority report and spent the night weeping and complaining against Moses and Aaron. Most of the people of Israel wanted to stone Joshua and Caleb. They were not an army; they were a lynch mob! Had it not been for the intercession of Moses, God would have totally destroyed them in their rebellion.[63]

One of Moses' most important tasks was to turn these slaves into soldiers and to organize the first Israelite army. To do this required that he change their thinking from that of slaves, to that of soldiers—a significant paradigm shift for Israel. In

---

[60] Exodus 2:23

[61] Exodus 4:22-23

[62] See Exodus chapters 5 through 15.

[63] See Numbers 13:26-14:34.

order to transform these slaves into soldiers in the army of *Jehovah Tsabaoth*, God told Moses to take a census of the whole community of Israel by their tribes, clans, and families. A list was made of the names of all the men twenty years old or older who were able to go to war. Moses and Aaron directed the project, assisted by one leader from each tribe.[64]

One of Moses' most important tasks was to turn these slaves into soldiers and to organize the first Israelite army. To do this required that he change their thinking from that of slaves, to that of soldiers.

"The military organization of the Israelites was based on the duty of every able-bodied male to bear arms and serve, whenever necessary, in his tribal contingent in the national hosts."[65] Thus, in Israel, men served in the army not only as citizens of the nation, but also as sons of a family, members of a tribe. The army protected the family and the family gave purpose to being in the army.

God called Israel out of Egypt because the nation was His beloved child, His son.[66] Not until they saw themselves as the Lord saw them would they become the soldiers needed to conquer the Promised Land. The masses saw themselves as grasshoppers—this was an insult to the God who had made them in His own image and had promised them this land!

Moses also had to change the Israelites' understanding of war. They perceived war as the destruction of the weak by the powerful. In ancient Israel, all of life was religious; all of life

---

[64] See Numbers 1:2-4.

[65] Chaim Herzog and Mordechai Gichon, *Battles of the Bible*, Greenhill Books, London revised edition 1997, p. 37.

[66] Hosea 11:1

was related to God. Warfare was no exception."[67] Holy war was to be seen as worship. And it was to be accomplished, *"not by might nor by power, but by My Spirit, says the LORD of hosts"*.[68]

Leaders

The courage of Israel's military leaders' was built, not on their self-confidence, brilliance or boldness, but on their faith in Israel's God. For example, Caleb and Joshua stood out from the crowd on the banks of the Jordan because these two wholly followed the Lord. [69]

Soldiers

When Israel was faithful, *Jehovah Tsabaoth* enabled the nation to win her military battles, as we see in the battle of Jericho[70] and the battle with the Amorites at Gibeon.[71] Sometimes when the odds were overwhelming and survival of His people was humanly impossible, God would defeat Israel's enemy without Israel doing any fighting. For example, at the time of the Exodus, there were as many as three million weaponless Israelites gathered on the banks of the Red Sea. But they saw themselves as slaves—not soldiers. Their number included women and children, the feeble, and the aged. They also had great herds of livestock. Looking to God, Moses told his

---

[67] Tremper Longman III and Daniel G. Reid, *God Is a Warrior,* Zondervan, Grand Rapids, MI, 1995, p. 32

[68] Zechariah 4:6b

[69] See Numbers 32:12.

[70] Joshua 6:2-5

[71] Joshua 10:12-14

people, *"The* LORD *will fight for you, and you shall hold your peace."*[72]

Later, as God through Moses formed Israel into an army, the twelve tribes were regarded as twelve military divisions prepared for battle under the direct leadership of *Jehovah*, the Divine Warrior. These divisions were to be composed of courageous, undistracted soldiers. They were to be free from domestic concerns—such as new homes, new brides and new businesses.[73] The fearful and fainthearted were not allowed to discourage others.[74]

Later when Saul became the first king of Israel, he paid little attention to the Lord's instruction in raising his first army. He used fear to manipulate 330,000 men to join his army.[75] Saul thought in terms of military war, not holy war. He wanted the

---

[72] Exodus 14:14. Two other examples of God defeating Israel's enemies without Israel fighting can be seen when King Hezekiah ruled in Judah (See 2 Chronicles 32:1-22 and Isaiah 37:1-37.) and in Jehoshaphat's battle with the people of Moab and Ammon (2 Chronicles 20:20-30).

[73] *"Then the officers shall speak to the people, saying: 'What man is there who has built a new house and has not dedicated it? Let him go and return to his house, lest he die in the battle and another man dedicate it. Also what man is there who has planted a vineyard and has not eaten of it? Let him go and return to his house, lest he die in the battle and another man eat of it. And what man is there who is betrothed to a woman and has not married her? Let him go and return to his house, lest he die in the battle and another man marry her.'"* (Deuteronomy 20:5-7)

[74] *"So it shall be, when you are on the verge of battle, that the priest shall approach and speak to the people. And he shall say to them, 'Hear, O Israel: Today you are on the verge of battle with your enemies. Do not let your heart faint, do not be afraid, and do not tremble or be terrified because of them; for the LORD your God is He who goes with you, to fight for you against your enemies, to save you.' The officers shall speak further to the people, and say, 'What man is there who is fearful and fainthearted? Let him go and return to his house, lest the heart of his brethren faint like his heart."* (Deuteronomy 20:2-4,8)

[75] See 1 Samuel 11:1-8.

biggest army possible. But God told Israel the principle of "superiority of numbers" did not apply to them. Through Moses, God had said, *"When you go out to battle against your enemies, and see horses and chariots and people more numerous than you, do not be afraid of them; for the LORD your God is with you, who brought you up from the land of Egypt."*[76]

Longman and Reid comment,
> One of the most interesting aspects of holy war is the relationship between God and the Israelite army. Since God fights for Israel, that nation does not have to worry about the number of its troops or its weapons. Indeed in the ethos of the Old Testament, a large army and superior weapons technology are a liability. Israel cannot boast in its own strength, but only in the might and power of the Lord, who gives victory in spite of overwhelming odds. It is better to go into battle with a small, poorly equipped army than with a large well-trained one. This is behind the story of Gideon (Judges 7). Thirty-two thousand men join him for battle but *"the LORD said to Gideon, 'The people who are with you are too many for Me to give the Midianites into their hands, lest Israel claim glory for itself against Me, saying, 'My own hand has saved me.'"* (Judges 7:2) Thus he allows all the troops who are afraid to return home. Nonetheless, he still has ten thousand left. Finally, an apparently arbitrary test was set up so that only three hundred troops would be chosen to participate in the battle.[77]

Another Old Testament illustration of the "little is much when God is in it" principle is the confrontation between David and

---

[76] Deuteronomy 20:1

[77] Tremper Longman III and Daniel G. Reid, *God Is a Warrior,* Zondervan, Grand Rapids, MI, 1995, p. 37.

Goliath.[78] David expressed holy war faith that all Israel was called to exhibit when he said to the Philistine:

> *You come to me with a sword, with a spear, and with a javelin. But I come to you in the name of the LORD of hosts, the God of the armies of Israel, whom you have defied. This day the LORD will deliver you into my hand, and I will strike you and take your head from you. And this day I will give the carcasses of the camp of the Philistines to the birds of the air and the wild beasts of the earth, that all the earth may know that there is a God in Israel. Then all this assembly shall know that the LORD does not save with sword and spear; for the battle is the LORD'S, and He will give you into our hands.*[79]

David's courage grew out of his past experience of God's faithfulness. So we see David bravely proceed to kill Goliath and cut off his head.

Organization

Joshua's army was organized with a very clear chain of command. *Jehovah Tsabaoth,* LORD of hosts, was the Commander-in-Chief of the Israeli army.[80] By His sovereign authority, He selected and called the covenant mediator, Moses. Under *Jehovah Tsabaoth,* the covenant mediator appointed the military leader, Joshua,[81] who then appointed leaders. God, through Moses, directed the officers to *"make captains of the armies to lead the people."*[82] Then these leaders appointed still other leaders.

---

78 See 1 Samuel 17.

79 1 Samuel 17:45-47

80 Joshua 5:14-15

81 Numbers 27:18-20

82 Deut. 20:9

Discipline was also present, although it was often imposed by God rather than as a result of self-discipline on the part of the Israelites. When the people doubted God and refused to enter the Promised Land, He refused to give them a second chance. Instead, He passed judgment on them with forty years of wandering in the wilderness, using this same experience to condition their children to be able to fight the battles necessary to conquer the Holy Land. On numerous occasions, when the people murmured against Moses, God repeatedly stepped in with judgment.

Intelligence

Moses, encamped at the oasis of Kadesh-barnea, needed to know about the land of Canaan beyond the miles of barren rock and sand of the Negev. To find out how best to go about conquering it, Moses sent out twelve spies.[83] However, the majority report terrified the people. They saw themselves as grasshoppers alongside the giants in the land and doubted their God's ability to give them the land He had promised. It is interesting to note that we seldom see spies or reconnaissance activity in the rest of the Old Testament. More often, God gave the tactics, and when Israel followed His directions, they were victorious.

Weapons

In holy war, Israel learned to place more confidence in the Lord than in their weapons. In Israel's battle with the Amalekites, Moses tells how Joshua overcame the enemy with the sword.[84] And yet, even though Israelite soldiers trained to become skillful at using their weapons, they were told not to depend on them for victory, but to trust the battle to God alone.

---

[83] See Numbers 13.

[84] Exodus 17:13

Even though each man used his sword to kill enemy soldiers, the success or failure of the battle lay in Moses' hands being continually lifted to the Lord in prayer.[85]

Holy War Model

Longman and Reid give us a three-division model for holy war. They describe what was required of Israel before the war, during the war, and after the war. Before the war, Israel was to seek God's will and make special preparation. In general, God revealed His will to the covenant mediator, who informed the nation. For example consider the conquest of the Promised Land.[86] When a specific battle situation arose, the war leader was to inquire of the Lord.[87] When on one occasion Joshua did not inquire of the Lord, he fell for the trickery of the Gibionites.[88]

Special spiritual preparation was necessary because holy war in the Bible is an act of worship. Sacrifices had to be offered before the battle.[89] It was in keeping with this that Joshua commanded his troops, *"Consecrate yourselves"*.[90] In obedience to this command, on the eve of the battle of Jericho, the whole army of Israel went through the rite of circumcision and celebrated Passover.[91]

During the war, Israel was to march, to carry the ark, and to remember they were not the sole combatants in their fight

---

[85] See Exodus 17:10-12.

[86] See Deuteronomy 7:1-2 and Joshua 5:13-15.

[87] For example, 1 Samuel 23:1-6 describes when David heard of the Philistine rape of the city of Keilah.

[88] See Joshua 9:14.

[89] See 1 Samuel 13.

[90] Joshua 3:5

[91] Compare this with Genesis 34.

against the enemy. God could have accomplished the conquest of the Promised Land with a single word, but He required Israel to march in and engage the enemy for three reasons. Their first-hand experience with God in the battle built their trust in Him; it demonstrated to their enemies that Israel belonged to the Lord; and it brought glory to God. In 2 Chronicles 20:20-23, the army sang praises to God during the march. This may have been a common occurrence in Israel's holy war.

The ark represented the presence of God with the army during warfare. It led the army day by day. Each night the ark was placed in the Tent of Meeting in the center of the camp.[92] The ark reminded the Israelites that they were combatants on the side of God, the Divine Warrior. [93] Along with God and Israel's army, there was also a third combatant, the heavenly army[94]—angelic beings who belong to the divine counsel.[95] The fourth ally with Israel was creation—a strong east wind,[96] hail stones,[97] the sun and moon,[98] and the stars.[99]

After the war, Israel was to praise God and plunder her defeated enemy. After God delivered the enemy to Israel, the only proper response was praise. Song was the primary vehicle for that expression.[100] Longman and Reid further note that the biblical phrase, "new song," is a term for victory. Just as the

---

[92] See Numbers 2.

[93] *"The LORD is a man of war; the LORD is His name."* Exodus 15:3

[94] See 2 Kings 6:17 and Joel 2:11.

[95] Daniel 10:21; 12:1; Revelation 12:7

[96] Exodus 14:21

[97] Joshua 10:9-11

[98] Joshua 10:1-15

[99] Judges 5:19-21

[100] See the Song of Moses in Exodus 15:1-15; also note that many Psalms grow out of war—see Psalm 7, Psalm 91 and Psalm 98.

victory belonged to God, so did the spoils of the war. This is why the Israelites obediently "burned the whole city" in offering to God.[101]

To summarize, *Jehovah Tsabaoth* is the Divine Warrior who alone could initiate holy war. The first Israeli army was built out of former slaves who saw themselves as grasshoppers. Not until they regained their understanding of what it meant to be sons did they become valiant soldiers. God called leaders for His people, and He demanded undistracted, courageous warriors. We saw the "little is much when God is in it" principle. Sometimes He chose to defeat Israel's enemy without Israel doing any fighting. God established a chain of command for authority and effectiveness and He enforced discipline. *Jehovah* usually provided the intelligence needed to defeat Israel's foes. God Himself fought as an ally with Israel, and so did the holy angels and all creation under His direction. Finally, holy war was regarded as an act of worship and it was to be prepared for, conducted, and celebrated accordingly.

Spiritual Warfare in the New Testament

Spiritual warfare described in the New Testament is a continuation of holy war in that God ordains it for the advancing of His kingdom, but it has two significant differences. In the Old Testament, God mandated Israel to use the sword to destroy the wicked, and to conquer and occupy the Promised Land, Palestine. In the New Testament, Christ commissioned the Church to use *"the sword of the Spirit, which is the word of God,"*[102] to *"make disciples of all the*

---

[101] Joshua 6:24. For a discussion of the devoted thing or the *herem,* see Tremper Longman III and Daniel G. Reid, *God Is a Warrior,* Zondervan, Grand Rapids, MI, pp. 46-47.

[102] Ephesians 6:17

nations."[103]   Holy war was physical and limited to one geographic location. Spiritual war is "spiritual" and embraces the whole world. Thus Christians are now allies with God in His conflict with the devil.

John White observes: "War is not something that illustrates aspects of Christian living. Christian living is war. Indeed I would go further. Earthly warfare is not the real war. It is but a faint, ugly reflection of the real thing. It is into the real war that the Christian is to plunge. Wars on earth are but tremors felt from an earthquake light-years away. The Christian's war takes place at the epicenter of the earthquake. It is infinitely more deadly, while the issues that hang on it make earth's most momentous questions no more than a village gossip."[104]

White continues, "The Holy Spirit uses the image of warfare to convey the nature of Christian living. No image could be more apt. The same courage, the same watchfulness, loyalty, endurance, resourcefulness, strength, skill, knowledge of the enemy, the same undying resolve to fight to the end come what may and at whatever cost must characterize Christian living as they do earthly warfare."[105]

The casualties of spiritual warfare are not reported as such in the daily newspaper. But the conflict between God and His angels and the devil and his demons is the ultimate war! What the devil did to Judas, he also desires to do to all Christians. First the devil deceived Judas, then he discredited him, and finally he destroyed him by suicide.

My wife's tearful voice on the other end of the phone exclaimed, "Andy is dead!" I sat in speechless unbelief. How

---

[103] Matthew 28:19.

[104] John White, *The Fight*, InterVarsity Press, Downers Grove, IL 1976, p. 216.

[105] Ibid.

could this be? I'd seen him in the coffee shop just a few days before. He talked about his work and his family. For twenty-five years, Andy had discipled men, now he had committed suicide. This act of desperation was preceded by a total unraveling of his life. His marriage had deteriorated to the point that his wife, after long and intensive counseling, had filed for divorce. Early one Saturday morning, he stretched out on a lawn chair in his yard and, after consuming a large amount of whiskey, put a shotgun to his head and pulled the trigger.

Over the weeks that followed, as I talked with his family and friends, a clearer picture formed of what brought Andy to his end. For years he had led a double life. He was one person with the men to whom he ministered; he was another man at home. His public image was one of piety and compassion, but his private life was one of control and selfishness. His work *for* God *became* his god. It seemed that he thought that if his marriage was over, so was his ministry. Anger had smoldered in him over a long period of time and this anger opened the door for the devil's deception.[106]   Andy was a casualty of spiritual warfare.

Many Christians don't even know there *is* a spiritual war! Their ignorance makes them more vulnerable. Everything visible and physical is the result of something invisible and spiritual.[107]   The visible battles with alcohol, drugs, fear or depression have a spiritual source, and thus they war with our passions and moral choices. Human beings, because they are God's image-bearers, have a formidable foe in the devil. He is the *"accuser of the brothers."*[108]   His plan is to attack believers

---

[106] See Ephesians 4:26-27.

[107] Tony Evans, *The Battle Is the Lord's: Waging Victorious Spiritual Warfare,* Moody Press, Chicago, IL, 1998, p. 10.

[108] Revelation 12:10

and *"detach us from dependency on God."*[109] He especially hates the family because it is the divinely ordained institution for multiplying men and women who bear the image of God and developing disciples and populating heaven.

Satan also hates the Church and seeks to destroy it by infiltrating it with *"doctrines of demons."*[110] The good news is that Christ has already won the victory! Satan has already been sentenced eternally for his sin of pride,[111] but he has two allies in the cosmic conflict: the flesh and the world. This means the believer has combat on three levels. We will deal with these enemies in greater detail later, but first, let's examine spiritual war using our military framework.

Many Christians don't even know there *is* a spiritual war! Their ignorance makes them more vulnerable.

Paradigm Shift

Very few Americans today have military experience and fewer still have actually engaged in combat. This makes it difficult for American Christians to grasp the implications of the spiritual warfare in which all believers are involved. Many Christians are like I was before I experienced combat in Korea; they are playing spiritual war-games but have yet to get into the real war. Alexander Whyte once said that to read John Bunyan's *Holy War* "kindles our cold civilian blood like the waving of a banner and like the sound of a trumpet."[112] As you

---

[109] Tony Evans, *The Battle Is the Lord's: Waging Victorious Spiritual Warfare,* Moody Press, Chicago, IL, 1998, p. 33.

[110] 1 Timothy 4:1

[111] Isaiah 14:15; Matthew 25:41

[112] Alexander Whyte, *Bunyan Characters, The Holy War,* Oliphant, Anderson and Ferrier, London, 1902, p. 12

read the balance of this book, ask the Lord to kindle your cold civilian blood and enable you to better understand the reality of the spiritual warfare in which all believers are engaged.

Christians must make a paradigm shift from a spiritual "civilian" to a spiritual "soldier." If you are a believer, you are a participant in holy war! Remember, a paradigm defines boundaries and tells us how to behave within the boundaries. To be successful in the civilian paradigm, we usually think in terms of wealth and power. For spiritual soldiers, however, success is the ability to do the whole will of God.[113]

Many Christians are like I was before I experienced combat in Korea; they are playing spiritual war-games but have yet to get into the real war.

As God raised up Moses to lead the people of Israel out of Egyptian bondage, so God raised up Christ to deliver His people from the bondage of sin *"into the glorious liberty of the children of God."*[114] Jesus said, *"I tell you the truth, everyone who sins is a slave to sin."*[115] Israel's bondage in Egypt was mild compared to the bondage of the human race in sin. When Jesus began His public ministry, He announced, *"The Spirit of the LORD is upon Me, because He has anointed Me to preach the gospel to the poor; He has sent Me to heal the brokenhearted, to proclaim liberty to the captives and recovery of sight to the blind, to set at liberty those who are oppressed."*[116] Jesus sets believers free from sin and by the

---

[113] See Joshua 1:7-8.
[114] Romans 8:21
[115] John 8:34
[116] Luke 4:18

Spirit of adoption He makes them sons and daughters of the Father.

Consciousness of this new relationship is essential in order for Christians to engage in spiritual warfare. Effective Christian soldiers must realize they are no longer slaves but sons, and if sons, then heirs of God through Christ.[117] Paul declared, *"For as many as are led by the Spirit of God, these are sons of God. For you did not receive the spirit of bondage again to fear, but you received the Spirit of adoption by whom we cry out, 'Abba, Father.' The Spirit Himself bears witness with our spirit that we are children of God, and if children, then heirs—heirs of God and joint heirs with Christ, if indeed we suffer with Him, that we may also be glorified together."*[118]

Paul learned to use the title *Abba* to address the Father from the teachings of Jesus. In the Lord's Prayer, Jesus authorizes His disciples to repeat the word *Abba* after Him. He gives them a share in His sonship and empowers them as His disciples to speak with their heavenly Father. John Knox said, "Prayer is an earnest and familiar talking with God to whom we make known our miseries, from whom we seek help, and to whom we give praise and thanks." [119] We may speak in just such a familiar, trusting way as a child would with his father. Jesus even goes so far as to say that it is this new relationship which first opens the door to God's reign, *"Truly I say to you, unless you are converted and become like children, you will not enter the kingdom of heaven."*[120]

When believers first cry *"Abba, Father,"* it is evidence of their sonship. But as they grow in the grace and knowledge of

---

[117] Galatians 4:7

[118] Romans 8:14-17

[119] W. Stanford Reid, *Trumpeter of God*, Charles Scribner's Sons, New York, 1974, p. 82.

[120] Matthew 18:3 NASB

Christ and actively participate in His army, their "cry" should also be their means of communication with their Commander-in-Chief. John Piper reminds us that prayer is not a domestic intercom between the den and the kitchen to order refreshment during halftime. Rather it is the warrior's walkie-talkie.[121] Adopted sons and daughters of God know they are soldiers in spiritual combat and seek to pray with kingdom-focus all the time about everything.

Early Christians had a strong self-consciousness of being "the people," "the laos," i.e., the *"chosen generation, a royal priesthood, a holy nation, His own special people."*[122] This self-consciousness was embedded in an equally strong knowledge that they were God's people solely by the grace of God. This consciousness was intimately related to the early Christians' understanding of what happened in baptism. Baptism was considered as a military oath. When Christians assumed their baptismal vows, they ceased to be civilians and became soldiers actively engaged in Christ's struggle for the kingdom.

The New Testament and the early Church never made a distinction between active and passive members. Every one was a missionary. And every baptized person had the authority and responsibility to be a missionary, for baptism and the accompanying unction were also considered as some kind of ordination. The writers of Scripture use many images or metaphors to describe the Church, but early Christians use only two modes to explain the Church's mission: the Church triumphant was composed of those saints who are now in glory, and the Church militant was composed of all believers still on earth. It was assumed that all believers on earth were

---

[121] John Piper, *Let the Nations Be Glad! The Supremacy of God in Missions,* Baker Books, Grand Rapids, MI, 1993, p. 46.

[122] 1 Peter 2:9

militant—actively involved in the spiritual war against the enemy.

Spiritual warfare cannot be successfully fought by men and women still enslaved to sin; only sons and daughters in a conscious vital relationship with their Father, and with His family in a local church, can properly serve as soldiers in Christ's army and gain victory in battles with the world, the flesh, and the devil. The primary task of pastors and other Christian leaders is to help former slaves of sin become valiant soldiers in the army of the Lord.[123]

The primary task of pastors and other Christian leaders is to help former slaves of sin become valiant soldiers in the army of the Lord.

Leaders

First, a word needs to be said about the key leader in the local church. Paul reminds us that the exalted Christ gave pastor-teachers, *"for the equipping of the saints for the work of ministry, for the edifying of the body of Christ."*[124] In the local church, it is the pastor-teacher who is responsible to equip the saints to be part of a healthy body, to be connected to other members—to receive and to give. As Paul encouraged Timothy, so the pastor should *"entrust to reliable men who will be qualified to teach others."*[125] Then when individuals are equipped, the pastor-teacher should delegate responsibility to them, just as Moses was instructed by his father-in-law to

---

[123] See John 8:34-35, Philippians 2:25 and 2 Timothy 2:3-4.
[124] See Ephesians 4:11-12.
[125] 2 Timothy 2:2 NIV

do.[126]   In this way, those people whom the pastor has equipped to be leaders will in turn equip still more leaders.

Neither the pastor nor the people he equips are required to be like military leaders. As spiritual warfare leaders, they need not have brilliant minds and strong bodies. Peter and John were, "uneducated and untrained men," who became bold because they had been with Jesus.[127] Paul, had infirmities but he boasted in them so that *"the power of Christ"* might rest upon him.[128] Paul urged believers in the Ephesian church to be, *"strong in the Lord and in the power of His might."*[129] And he exhorted young Timothy to be *"strong in the grace that is in Christ Jesus."*[130] Paul goes so far as to say that he could *"do all things through Christ who strengthens"* him.[131]

Leaders in spiritual warfare should be courageous. It was said of John Knox that he feared God too much to fear any man. The courage of spiritual warriors is built, not on human brilliance or boldness, but on confidence in the God of Abraham, Isaac, and Jacob, the Father of our Lord Jesus Christ.

Leaders in spiritual warfare lead by example, and humbly urge others to follow them as they follow Christ. They are flawed human beings who recognize their shortcomings and seek to deal with them. The virtues listed by Paul for leaders are their ideals, and to these they constantly aspire. Whenever they become aware of sin in their hearts and lives, they deal with it.

---

[126] Exodus 18:13-23

[127] Acts 4:13

[128] See 2 Corinthians 12:9-10.

[129] Ephesians 6:10

[130] See 2 Timothy 2:1.

[131] Philippians 4:13. See also Proverbs 28:1; Psalm 138:3 and Hebrews 4:16.

Spiritual warfare leaders seek to be effective and efficient, but their confidence is in the Lord and not in their own abilities. They must be people of prayer. They see the Church as a prayer-driven, militant, mighty army. They do not think of the Church as a peacetime business, needing only efficient management. They are willing to suffer, and to move ahead with joyful determination. They are risk-takers, launching out by faith in God alone. They are not dictators; rather they are humble, servant-leaders.

Our Lord showed us how to be servant-leaders.[132] John tells us, *"So when He had washed their feet, taken His garments, and sat down again, He said to them, 'Do you know what I have done to you? You call me Teacher and Lord, and you say well, for so I am. If I then, your Lord and Teacher, have washed your feet, you also ought to wash one another's feet. For I have given you an example, that you should do as I have done to you.'"*[133]   (Local church leadership is considered more fully in the third book in the Kingdom Campaign series, **Invigorate Your Church**.)

Soldiers

Soldiers in spiritual warfare must be good followers.   The writer of Hebrews exhorts, *"Remember your leaders, who spoke the word of God to you. Consider the outcome of their way of life and imitate their faith."*[134]   The Apostle Paul introduces the soldier and fellow-soldier as images of Christians performing tasks under authority.   All three occurrences of the term *soldier* are found in letters that Paul wrote from prison, surrounded by Roman soldiers. He refers to Epaphrodites[135] and to Archipes[136] as fellow soldiers. He urges

---

[132] See Mark 9:33-37.
[133] John 13:12-15
[134] Hebrews 13:7 NIV
[135] Philippians 2:25

Timothy, *"Endure hardship with us like a good soldier of Christ Jesus. No one serving as a soldier gets involved with civilian affairs—he wants to please his commanding officer."*[137]

Spiritual warfare is unlike military warfare in which the army with the most, and strongest, soldiers usually wins the battle. Spiritual warfare, like holy warfare, requires only a small number of undistracted and strong-hearted warriors following their leaders as the leaders follow *Jehovah Tsabaoth.* They are invincible! Like the human leaders they follow, they know they are flawed beings. They too recognize their shortcomings and seek to deal with them. They too seek to develop the virtues listed by Paul, as they see them fleshed out in their leaders. They, too, deal with sin whenever they become aware of it.

In both military and spiritual warfare, maintaining high morale among the troops is essential if they are to fight valiantly. This is well illustrated in the crucial battles of the Reformation. Reid tells us:

> The Calvinist reformers were led by a militant aristocracy and financed by wealthy bourgeoisie, they put up a long and frequently successful battle. Yet the leadership and finance could not have won the day had the individual Calvinists not possessed, to quote Cromwell, "a conscience of what they were doing." In many cases, they won their battles or retrieved those they had lost, not through generalship nor through greater economic power, but because of superior morale. In building up and maintaining this morale, the battle hymns of the Psalter played a conspicuous part.

---

[136] Philemon 2

[137] 2 Timothy 2:3-4 NIV

The psalms owed their importance in this connection primarily to Calvin himself. Usually when thinking of all his influence on the resistance movements, we tend to stress his teachings, his organization, and his personality. Yet at the grass-roots level these perhaps did not have all of the impact, which we usually attribute to them. The thing that really "grabbed" the common man, the ordinary Calvinistic soldier, was something much more mundane: *his catechetical training*[138] *and the congregational singing of the psalms.* More than all the fine theological reasoning, both the catechism and the Psalter entered into the fabric of the humblest members' lives. For this the credit must largely go to the first pastor of Geneva.[139]

When soldiers in spiritual warfare enter into battles following the Lord's guidance, He enables them to accomplish what He desires. But like ancient Israel, they must engage the enemy before He grants the victory. As Christians enter the spiritual battles, three things happen: their confidence in the Lord grows, the Church's enemies know that the Church belongs to the Lord, and God is glorified.

Organization

When we considered military warfare, we saw that fundamental organization, including the chain of command and

---

[138] The use of question and answer instruction used in Catechisms was part of the Passover celebration. See Exodus 12:25-27: *"When you enter the land that the LORD will give you as he promised, observe this ceremony. And when your children ask you, 'What does this ceremony mean to you?' then tell them, 'It is the Passover sacrifice to the LORD, who passed over the houses of the Israelites in Egypt and spared our homes when he struck down the Egyptians.'"*

[139] W. Stanford Reid, "The Battle Hymns of the Lord, Calvinist Psalmody of the Sixteen Century," Journal of Modern History, pp 36-54.

discipline, make the difference between an army and armed rabble. Much can be said for and against organization; let me admit the danger of organization that is so efficient that we tend to rely on ourselves and fail to rely on the Lord. Nevertheless, Scripture makes it abundantly clear that God is organized. We see this first in the Godhead itself. The Father sends both the Son and the Holy Spirit; the Son proceeds from the Father and sends the Holy Spirit; and the Holy Spirit proceeds from both the Father and the Son. Second, the created universe reflects an organized Creator! The human body is an amazingly organized organism. God designed families with parents in charge of their children, and with the husband as the head of the family. Third, God created the heavenly angelic army and organized them into ranks with specific functions.[140] Fourth, we saw that God also organized Israel into an army to fight His holy war.

For the Church to be victorious in spiritual warfare, it needs proper organization. The first requirement is that we must truly submit to Christ, the Head of the Church, as our Commander-in-Chief. Then we must see the order He has established so that His Church can be a victorious army. Christ *"Himself gave some to be apostles, some prophets, some evangelists, and some pastors and teachers, for the equipping of the saints for the work of ministry, for the edifying of the body of Christ."*[141] Paul indicates that Church leaders have authority. He said to the Thessalonians, *"We urge you, brethren, to recognize those who labor among you, and are over you in the Lord and admonish you, and to esteem them very highly in love for their work's sake. Be at peace among*

---

[140] Different ranks: are seen in the seraphs (Isaiah 6:2), archangels (1 Thessalonians 4:16), angels, authorities and powers (1 Peter 3:22), and archangel Michael and his angels (Jude 1:9 and Revelation 12:7).

[141] Ephesians 4:11-12

yourselves."[142] And the writer of Hebrews explains further, *"Obey your leaders and submit to their authority. They keep watch over you as men who must give an account. Obey them so that their work will be a joy, not a burden, for that would be of no advantage to you."*[143]

Most modern American local churches elect official leaders or have them appointed, but they have little or no additional effective organization. This is one reason why the vast majority of all local churches have less than 100 active attending members. The Jews of Jesus' day did not recognize a synagogue as legitimate unless it had at least 120 active members.[144] The family is the ideal substructure for local churches. But the condition of the American Christian family is such that it needs the local church to organize an equipping process that will help parents, especially fathers, to establish their families as outposts of heaven for spiritual warfare. In heaven, when the entire Church militant becomes the Church triumphant, the Church will no longer need to be an army. Then she will be the family and God will not be the Commander-in-Chief, but the Father. Let me underscore, that even in this world the church does not replace family, but facilitates and complements it. (This is discussed further in *Intercede For and With Your Family*.)

If the church is to be an army, it must have basic organization, a chain of encouragement, and disciplined, fearless fighters who are not entangled *"with the affairs of this life."*[145] Paul disciplined his body and brought it into subjection, lest, when

---

[142] 1 Thessalonians 5:12-13

[143] Hebrews 13:17

[144] "The number of officers in a community must be 1/10th of the whole, and 120 is the smallest number which can hold a 'small Sanhedrin.'" Sanhedrin 1:6

[145] 2 Timothy 2:4

he had preached to others, he should become disqualified.[146] The discipline necessary for winning spiritual battles is even more demanding than the discipline required for winning military battles. It grows out of devotion to Christ and love for His people.[147] It leads to the highest level of dedication of individual believers and groups of believers. This devotion to Christ and love for His people produces twenty-four-hour-a-day loving obedience. Devotion-driven discipline cannot be imposed from the outside, but rather it grows as the heart surrenders to the crucified, resurrected, ascended, and returning Lord. This devotion-driven discipline does not come from a deep, internal need to excel, but from the passion to glorify the Lord. It is this devotion-driven discipline that enables Christians to do the right thing, even when it is not the natural thing to do.

Intelligence

General "Chesty" Puller was the only marine in history to win five Navy Cross citations. Many considered him too tough for the Marine Corps. Anticipating the fighting in Korea he once said, "Never underestimate the enemy. If you don't figure him to have as much sense as you've got, you'll have trouble."[148]

As our troop ship plowed through the fringe of a Pacific typhoon on its way to Korea, we were issued manuals titled, *Know Your Enemy*. These manuals described the typical North Korean soldier, his weapons, and his tactics. For more than two years I had played war games and fought theoretical aggressors. Now this manual identified the enemy that I would soon see face-to-face. This manual was helpful, but it was inadequate—because it did not tell us how to identify a North

---

[146] See 1 Corinthians 9:27.

[147] See Philippians. 1:21 and 1 John 4:7-11.

[148] Burke Davis, *Marine! The Life of Chesty Puller, The Only Marine in History to Win Five Navy Crosses*, Bantam Books, New York, 1964, p. 238.

Korean soldier out of uniform from a South Korean civilian. The manual did not tell us that the North Korean soldiers would give little children backpacks filled with hand grenades and send them into our ranks. And, the manual never told us about the more than 500,000 Chinese soldiers that would enter the battle from Manchuria. The manual said nothing about the bitter, twenty-to-thirty-below-zero temperatures we would face in this land of the Mongols.

The Church as an army needs spiritual intelligence. This world is enemy territory. Local churches should study the areas around their buildings to discover what is needed to release the spiritual prisoners of war close at hand. Christian families and individuals need to study the neighborhoods around where they live and work. (This will be explored further in *Impact Your World*.) But as we study our areas, we should put in an equal amount of time getting to know our God better. If we do not, we will make the same mistake that the ten spies made—we will seem like grasshoppers in our own eyes.

In spiritual war, believers must know our enemies and fortunately, we have a manual that gives us all the information we need to win life's battles—the Bible. As we listen to God speaking through His word, we will not engage the enemy in self-reliance, nor will we try to use force to conquer our territory, like Israel did to conquer Palestine. We will, through kingdom-focused prayer, battle for healthy Christian families, vital churches, and a godly nation—the three institutions ordained by God. But the most strategic battles to be fought will be those of personal godliness, for it will determine our ability to function with integrity within these institutions.

In spiritual war, believers must know our enemies and fortunately, we have a manual that gives us all the information we need to win life's battles—the Bible.

Weapons

Military warfare needs the most and the best weapons that technology can produce. Holy warfare uses a wide variety of weapons, but for victory, the warrior trusts *Jehovah Tsabaoth*, not his weapons. In contrast with both, spiritual warfare requires spiritual weapons. The Apostle Paul explains, *"For though we walk in the flesh, we do not war according to the flesh. For the weapons of our warfare are not carnal but mighty in God for pulling down strongholds, casting down arguments and every high thing that exalts itself against the knowledge of God, bringing every thought into captivity to the obedience of Christ."*[149]

Though there are significant differences between the devil, the world, and the flesh, our chief weapon against them all is one-and-the-same—prayer. John White correctly states, "Hell's legions are terrified of prayer. Satan trembles when he sees the weakest saint upon his knees."[150] Hell was so fearful of Daniel's resolve to pray that we read of all-out attack in the heavenlies on his prayer. An angelic visitor told the trembling prophet: *"'Do not fear, Daniel, for from the first day that you set your heart to understand, and to humble yourself before your God, your words were heard; and I have come because of your words.' But the prince of the kingdom of Persia withstood me twenty-one days; and behold, Michael, one of the chief princes, came to help me, for I had been left alone there with the kings of Persia."*[151]

Jesus taught us to pray, *"Your kingdom come. Your will be done on earth as it is in heaven."*[152] This petition makes it

---

[149] 2 Corinthians 10:3-5

[150] John White, *The Fight*, InterVarsity Press, Downers Grove, IL 1976, p. 218.

[151] Daniel 10:12-13

[152] Matthew 6:10

clear—for Jesus, the Christian life is spiritual warfare. Two wills (*Jehovah's* and Satan's) are in irreconcilable conflict. Two kingdoms are in conflict, the kingdom of God and the kingdom of the devil. The petition, *"Thy kingdom come,"* is a cry for the coming of a radical new order, one in which righteousness rules. This prayer is a call to arms and is in itself a mighty weapon to achieve victory. The fact that Jesus, the Son of God, provides this prayer gives us certainty that it will be answered. There is no weapon in the devil's arsenal that can counter it. O. Hallesby tells us, "The secret prayer chamber is a bloody battleground. Here bloody and decisive battles are fought out."[153]

Though there are significant differences between the devil, the world, and the flesh, our chief weapon against them all is one-and-the-same—prayer.

Kingdom-focused prayer is a spiritual super-weapon. We learn how to develop and use it by observing Jesus and listening to His words. Scripture tells us, *"In the days of His flesh, when He had offered up prayers and supplications, with vehement cries and tears to Him who was able to save Him from death, and was heard because of His godly fear."*[154] Jesus' life was one of prayer from the launching of his public ministry to its climax—from Satan's testing in the wilderness, to His agony in the garden of Gethsemane, and His suffering on the cross. It was not an isolated incident of prayer that caused one of His disciples to ask, *"Lord, teach us to pray."*[155] By His example, Jesus Christ demonstrated the necessity of prayer. "If in His

---

[153] O. Hallesby, *Prayer,* Augsburg Fortress Publishers, Minneapolis, MN, 1931, p. 98.
[154] Hebrews 5:7-8
[155] Luke 11:1

life there was not only room but need for prayer, much more must there be room and need in such lives as ours."[156]

The early Church moved forward by kingdom-focused prayer.[157] A major part of this prayer was corporate. Most of the early Christians were devout Jews. As devout Jews, they considered the Psalms to be God's inspired prayer book and their battle hymns. A study of quotations from the Old Testament in the New Testament shows that more verses are quoted from the Psalms than any other book.[158] It was nothing unusual for them to know "the whole of David" by heart. The Psalter shaped the prayer life of early Christianity into a militant kingdom focus. God gave concord of many hearts in prayer and He moved in mighty power.

By His example, Jesus Christ demonstrated the necessity of prayer. "If in His life there was not only room but need for prayer, much more must there be room and need in such lives as ours."

Today's Church needs to rebuild and use its super-weapon, kingdom-focused prayer. The apostles said, *"We will devote ourselves to prayer, and to the ministry of the word."*[159] God said, *"Fire shall be kept burning continually on the altar; it is*

---

[156] Alfred Plummer, *Commentary on the Gospel of Luke*, T&T Clark, Edinburgh, 1960, p. 391.

[157] See Acts 4:23-31; 6:4; 7:59-60; 9:4-6,10-16; 10:9-15; 10:30-31; 11:5-14; 12:5-12; 13:2-3; 14:23; 16:13-15; 16:16-18; 20:36; and 28:8-9.

[158] Nestlé-Aland, *Novum Testamentum Graece*, Deuche Biblestifung, Stuttgart, Germany, 1979, pp. 752-57; 758-62. 371 passages from Isaiah are found in 590 New Testament passages and 426 passages from Psalms are quoted in 565 New Testament passages.

[159] Acts 6:4 NASB

not to go out."[160]   This fire represents the ministry of intercession. The Old Testament priests were to keep the fires of intercession burning at all times. With Christ's finished work on the cross, the curtain in the temple was ripped apart, signifying that God's people could now enter the throne room of God because of Christ's bloody propitiation for our sins. Peter declared, *"You are a chosen race, a royal priesthood"*[161]—all believers now are priests who are to keep the fires of intercession burning at all times.

Ezekiel said of his generation, *"They have blown the trumpet and made everyone ready, but no one goes to battle; for My wrath is on all their multitude."*[162] Like Ezekiel's generation, the American Church today needs a new heart for the spiritual battle. We must *not* be like Israel in Egypt, dominated by pagan taskmasters. We must *not* be like Israel in the desert murmuring against authority and discipline. Let us, like Joshua, be willing, undistracted, whole-hearted soldiers of the cross.

To summarize, Christian living is spiritual warfare. Christians are now caught in the crossfire of an invisible conflict between God and His angels, and the devil and his demons. Scripture presents the kingdom of God as already here spiritually as Christ reigns in the hearts of His people. Scripture also presents the kingdom of God as yet to come in the final sense when all the kingdoms of the earth shall become the kingdom of our God and of His Christ. The deciding battle has been fought and won at Calvary. The outcome of the war is certain; nevertheless, we are still in ongoing battles while we wait for the consummation of all things. The Bible has given us what

---

[160] Leviticus 6:13 NASB

[161] 1 Peter 2:9 NASB

[162] Ezekiel 7:14

we need to know in order to be victorious in our remaining battles.

> **Christian living is spiritual warfare. That in which we are engaged may seem less concrete and tangible than was Israel's holy war for Canaan, but it is no less real and urgent.**

Only men and women set free from sin through faith in Christ can successfully fight spiritual warfare. As sons and daughters in a conscious vital relationship with our Father and with His family in a local church, we can properly serve as soldiers in Christ's army and gain victory in battles with the world, the flesh, and the devil. Leaders in spiritual warfare need not be brilliant; they cannot be self-confident. They are to be humble servants, who are courageous because they are confident in the Lord. They lead by example, and are people of prayer, who multiply after their kind. Soldiers in spiritual warfare are humble followers of Jesus who maintain their morale by a steady diet of psalms and basic Christian truth, especially Scripture. They boldly engage the enemy. Spiritual warfare requires a chain of encouragement and discipline. Spiritual warriors know their enemies and believe God is sufficient to defeat them. Spiritual warriors believe kingdom-focused prayer is their super-weapon.

Until the end of time, the Church will continue in spiritual war. Certainly the present plight of the Church indicates that a supernatural, spiritual battle is raging. Hence, the times demand that we as Christians stand our ground and not give another inch to the enemy! It is time to follow the Holy Spirit's guidance through biblical principles to organize the Church for spiritual warfare. The Kingdom Campaign provides a strategy based on the spiritual warfare model to gather God's people into a spiritual army, building and using our super-weapon, kingdom-focused prayer.[163]   To fight the battles of this spiritual war, pastors and church leaders must first see the "big picture"—that Christian life is war, and they must lead the Church to fight until the end of time.   The combat force is to be made up of *all* able-spirited Christians, functioning in fireteams that engage and destroy the forces of evil through intercessory prayer. Jesus promised, *"Again I say to you that if two of you agree on earth concerning anything that they ask, it will be done for them by My Father in heaven."*[164]   The spiritual warfare in which we are engaged may seem less concrete and tangible than was Israel's holy war for Canaan, but it is no less real and urgent.

Having gained insights from the holy war model of the Old Testament and spiritual warfare of the New Testament we should now have a greater sense of urgency about our role as prayer warriors—kingdom intercessors.   So let us turn to the task of learning more about how we can improve our prayer lives.

The times demand that we as Christians stand our ground and not give another inch to the enemy!

•••••

---

[163] For more information, please see the booklet, ***The Kingdom Campaign***, available from Serve International.

[164] Matthew 18:19

Basic Training

Is your prayer life as effective as it should be? I have surveyed more than 6,000 people with this question. Only one said, "Yes!" He later told me he misunderstood the question.

Reasons for dissatisfaction with one's prayer life are varied. Bill told me, "I seldom sense God's presence when I pray." Ashley said, "Occasionally God answers my prayers but most of the things I ask for never happen." Chuck admitted, "I pray daily for my family and for the work of my church but this has become just another habit."   And Jim confessed, "I pray because I know I'm supposed to, but I seldom find it joyful." Dissatisfaction is one of the major reasons the majority of the 6,000 Christian leaders and workers who completed the survey spend less than fifteen minutes a day in prayer.

When I found myself at a point of dissatisfaction with my life, a few close friends covenanted to pray and fast with me for three days to help me discover what God was trying to tell me. At the end of these three days, I could see that God was just beginning a new work in me. So, for a total of four weeks I continued my fast, reading the word and praying. As I pillowed my head the last few nights I was not sure I would wake up in this world. And I instinctively found myself praying, "Now I lay me down to sleep. I pray the Lord my soul to keep. If I should die before I wake, I pray the Lord my soul to take."

During this period, my perspective on life changed radically! God's presence was more delightful. Experiencing the frailty of my flesh enabled me to better see the importance of the spiritual. The Spirit focused my gaze on thirty years of work—not what I had done—but *why* and *how* I had done the work. Often I had used the methods of the American corporate world—its management and marketing techniques, and the salesman's principles of persuasion. Now God's message to me was, "Archie, your work for Me is a poor substitute for My work in and through you."

Is your prayer life as effective as it should be?

As I mentioned earlier, my training for ministry concentrated on making me a man of the word. Through my entire ministry, I prayed, but I never became a man of prayer. The Apostles said, *"We will give ourselves continually to prayer and to the ministry of the word."*[165]   Only when the word and prayer *proportionately* complement each other does God release the fullness of His gracious power. The error I made for most of my life, the error which the majority of Christian leaders today make, is simply this — not spending as much time in prayer as is spent in study. Study should not become less, but prayer must become more. Sometimes when preaching and teaching lack anointing, it is because there is not enough effectual prayer. Paul Cho is pastor of the largest church in the world in Seoul, Korea. I once heard him say, "When I see someone yawn as I preach, I know that I have not prayed enough."

Lord, Teach Us to Pray

Prayer is both a divine gift and a human activity. The first principle for improving one's prayer life is to ask God to help us pray. "All progress in prayer is an answer to prayer—our

---

[165] Acts 6:4

own or another's. And all true prayer promotes its own progress and increases our power to pray."[166] Divine help will give us our focus on the kingdom of God. When one of Jesus' disciples asked, *"Lord, teach us to pray,"*[167] Jesus answered the disciple's request for more powerful prayer by giving us what is now generally called the "Lord's Prayer." The early Christians called it "The Prayer." It is our pattern prayer and it is radical! In this prayer, Jesus provided many new insights.

Prayer is both a divine gift and a human activity. The first principle for improving one's prayer life is to ask God to help us pray.

Savonarola petitioned, "Enlighten, enflame me, teach me what I ought to pray."[168] Why do we need to be taught to pray? As Jesus' disciples watched Him pray, they realized their need to be more effective in prayer. One of them asked, *"Lord, teach us to pray."*[169] The disciple's request did not mean that he had no knowledge or experience of prayer. The Jews in Jesus' day had a fixed pattern for prayer that was a discipline from early childhood.

Josephus the Jewish historian tells us, "Twice a day, at the beginning and when the hour of sleep approaches, it is fitting to remember in gratitude before God the gifts which He gave us after the deliverance from Egypt.[170] This they did by reciting what Jewish people everywhere considered their creed, the

---

[166] P. T. Forsyth, *The Soul of Prayer,* Eerdmans Publishing, Grand Rapids, MI, 1916, p. 11

[167] Luke 11:1

[168] Fredrick Heiler, *Prayer, A Study In the History and Psychology of Religion*, Oxford University Press, London, 1932, p. 110.

[169] Luke 11:1

[170] Flavius Josephus, *The Jewish Antiquities 4.212.*

Shema. *"Hear, O Israel: The LORD our God, the LORD is one!"*[171] To these words was added: *"You shall love the LORD your God with all your heart, with all your soul, and with all your strength. And these words which I command you today shall be in your heart. You shall teach them diligently to your children, and shall talk of them when you sit in your house, when you walk by the way, when you lie down, and when you rise up. You shall bind them as a sign on your hand, and they shall be as frontlets between your eyes. You shall write them on the doorposts of your house and on your gates."*[172]

All men and boys after their twelfth birthday recited this expanded creed regularly. Probably because of the words, *"when you lie down, and when you rise up,"* it was recited between dawn and sunrise each morning and the last thing each night.

In addition to the reciting of this creed, as early as the time of Daniel, there were three fixed periods of daily prayer. *"Now when Daniel knew that the writing was signed, he went home. And in his upper room, with his windows open toward Jerusalem, he knelt down on his knees three times that day, and prayed and gave thanks before his God, as was his custom since early days."*[173]

The prayer used on these occasions was called the *Tephilla* that is, the grand benediction. It is a hymn consisting of a string of benedictions. At the end of the first century the number was fixed at eighteen and so the *Tephilla* is also called the "eighteen benedictions". These benedictions were among the specific prayers that devout Jews learned by heart. To these

---

[171] Deuteronomy 6:4

[172] Deuteronomy 6:5-9

[173] Daniel 6:10. Psalm 55:17, *"Evening and morning and at noon I will pray, and cry aloud, and He shall hear my voice,"* also reflects three periods of daily prayer.

benedictions each man, woman or slave added his or her own private petitions. Devoted Jews today still pray according to these long-standing customs.[174]

To these five periods of prayer, the practice of grace said before each meal and blessing after each meal was added. The *Talmud*, which contains ancient traditions of the Jews, tells us that a blessing for food was first articulated by Moses in gratitude for the manna that the Israelites ate in the desert.[175] The ancient rabbis taught, "It is forbidden to a man to enjoy anything of this world without a benediction, and if anyone enjoys anything of this world without a benediction, he commits sacrilege."[176] It would be the same as taking something that doesn't belong to us without the permission of the owner. This is so because no aspect of life is devoid of God's presence. *"The earth is the LORD'S, and everything in it, the world, and all who live in it."*[177] The Jewish sages prescribed blessings to say before eating. It mattered not if one ate a full dinner or a casual snack. The oldest and most universal of the Jewish blessings is:

Blessed art Thou, Lord our God, King of the universe, who in His goodness, grace, loving kindness, and mercy, nourishes the whole world. He gives food to all flesh, for His loving kindness is everlasting. In His great goodness, we have never lacked for food; may we never lack for food, for the sake of His great Name. For He nourishes and sustains all, He does good to all, and prepares food for all His creatures that He created. Blessed art Thou, Lord, who provides food for all.[178]

---

[174] See Hayim Halevy Donin, *To Pray as a Jew,* HarperCollins, New York, 1980, "Prayers in the Home," p. 284 ff.

[175] For a description, see Exodus 16:14 ff.

[176] *Babylonian Talmud*, Berakoth, 35a.

[177] Psalm 24:1 NIV

[178] Marvin R. Wilson, *Our Father Abraham, Jewish Roots of the Christian Faith,* Eerdmans Publishing, Grand Rapids, MI. 1989, pgs. 157-158.

Moses commanded, *"When you have eaten and are satisfied, praise the* LORD *your God for the good land he has given you."*[179] The biblical duty is to recite a blessing after eating because when people are satisfied, they are more likely to forget Him who is the source of their refreshment. It is easier to think of God and be grateful to Him when the food is still before us and we are hungry. It often happens that when people are able comfortably to meet their basic needs, they turn away from God.

There is no need to bless the actual food or drink. The blessing does not transfer holiness to the object itself, but rather entitles us to properly partake of the world's pleasure. We focus our prayer on blessing God, the Creator and Giver. We give thanks to the Lord and thereby acknowledge that the earth is His and we are its caretakers. Jesus followed this custom.[180] The blessings before eating or drinking are part of a broader category of *blessings of enjoyment*, said for things that bring pleasure.

Thus with the *Shema* in the morning and evening, the three periods of prayer built around the *Tephilla*, and the grace before and the blessing after each meal, the normal Jewish day was punctuated with eleven times for prayer.

So the disciple's request, *"Lord, teach us to pray,"*[181] was not an indication that he was ignorant of prayer. Rather it had other implications. In asking Jesus for help, the disciple is praying for his ability to pray. He admitted that something in Jesus' praying went beyond his knowledge and experience.

---

[179] Deuteronomy 8:10 NIV
[180] See Matthew 26:26 and Luke 24:30.
[181] Luke 11:1

Also he was asking Jesus for a specific prayer that would reflect the fact that the one who prayed it was a follower of Jesus. Jeremias expresses it this way; "Now the disciple desires Jesus give them a fixed prayer which will correspond to His message. In essence he asks, 'Teach us to pray as men who are already partakers of the coming reign of God.'" [182] John the Baptist taught such prayers to his followers; Jesus' disciples now ask Him to do the same for them. *"So He said to them, 'When you pray, say: Our Father in heaven, hallowed be Your name. Your kingdom come. Your will be done on earth as it is in heaven. Give us day by day our daily bread. And forgive us our sins, for we also forgive everyone who is indebted to us. And do not lead us into temptation, but deliver us from the evil one.'"* [183]

The kingdom of God is the central focus of the Lord's Prayer. Bible scholars agree that the central theme of both Old and New Testaments is the kingdom of God. But exactly what that kingdom is, and how it is manifested are subjects of wide disagreement. When the disciples ask Jesus, *"'Lord, will You at this time restore the kingdom to Israel?' And He said to them, 'It is not for you to know times or seasons which the Father has put in His own authority. But you shall receive power when the Holy Spirit has come upon you; and you shall be witnesses to Me in Jerusalem, and in all Judea and Samaria, and to the end of the earth.'"* [184] For our present purpose, we need not get into "times or seasons" of the kingdom. Rather, we will focus on the spiritual essence of the kingdom on which most evangelical believers would agree. John Bright says to pray, *"Thy kingdom come,"* is to pray

---

[182] Joachim Jeremias, *The Prayers of Jesus,* Studies in Biblical Theology, Second Series 6, London: SCM, 1967; Philadelphia: Fortress, 1979, p. 73.

[183] Luke 11:2-4

[184] Acts 1:6-8

precisely that the rule of God triumph everywhere."[185] George Ladd amplifies this thought. He expresses the meaning of "kingdom" in the petition, *"Thy kingdom come,"* with these words:

> Are we praying for heaven to come to earth? In a sense we are praying for this; but heaven is an object of desire only because the reign of God is to be more perfectly realized than it is now. Apart from the reign of God, heaven is meaningless. Therefore, what we pray for is, *"Thy kingdom come; Thy will be done on earth as it is in heaven."* This prayer is a petition for God to reign, to manifest His kingly sovereignty and power, to put to flight every enemy of righteousness and of His divine rule, that God alone may be King over all the world.[186]

We pray, *"Thy kingdom come, Thy will be done on earth as it is in heaven."* The confidence that this prayer is to be answered when God brings human history to the divinely ordained consummation enables the Christian to retain his balance and sanity of mind in this mad world in which we live. Our hearts go out to those who have no such hope. Thank God, His kingdom is coming, and it will fill all the earth.

We should also pray, *"Thy kingdom come, Thy will be done"* <u>in my church</u> as it is in heaven. The life and fellowship of a Christian church ought to be a fellowship of people among whom God's will is done—a bit of heaven on earth. *"Thy kingdom come, Thy will be done"* <u>in my life</u> as it is in heaven. This is included in our

---

[185] John Bright, *The Kingdom of God,* Abingdon Press, Nashville, TN, 1953, p. 262.

[186] George Ladd, *The Gospel of the Kingdom,* Eerdmans Publishing, Grand Rapids, MI, 1959, p. 21.

prayer for the coming of the kingdom. This is part of the gospel of the kingdom of God.[187]

Yes, the kingdom of God is the central focus of the Lord's Prayer. As this has historically been considered "the pattern prayer," all prayer should be kingdom-focused. I define kingdom-focused prayer as the Spirit-enabled, reverent cry of God's adopted children, seeking their Father's glory by persistently asking Him for the nations, their promised inheritance.

Kingdom-focused prayer is the Spirit-enabled, reverent cry of God's adopted children, seeking their Father's glory by persistently asking Him for the nations, their promised inheritance.

Prayer is a divine gift. To improve your prayer life, you must begin by asking God to help you pray, as He desires you to pray. But, as we'll see next, prayer is also a human activity, an essential part of exercising yourself toward godliness.

Exercise Yourself Toward Godliness

Scripture says to *"exercise yourself toward godliness. For bodily exercise profits a little, but godliness is profitable for all things, having promise of the life that now is and of that which is to come."*[188]

Prayer is a universal human instinct. When God is all you have, it is basic instinct to call out to Him with all that you

---

[187] George Ladd, *The Gospel of the Kingdom,* Eerdmans Publishing, Grand Rapids, MI, 1959, p. 23.

[188] 1 Timothy 4:7-8

have. Saint Augustine considered the best disposition for praying to be that of being desolate, forsaken, stripped of everything. Prayer is natural to all human beings. As Abraham Kuyper explains, "The possibility of prayer finds its deepest ground in the fact of our being created after the image of God. From this fact springs the mighty truth that I, as a human being, can be conscious of the existence of the Eternal. I can be conscious of the intimate bond and relation that manifests itself in prayer as soon as I address God."[189]

Prayer is a universal human instinct, natural to all human beings.

"Thus prayer is the drawing and pressing of the impressed image toward its Original, which is the three-in-one God. Owing its origin to the impress of that Original Image, our inward being draws toward God—naturally, urgently, and persistently. Our inward being cannot live without relating to its Creator. However, prayer is not an involuntary action like a rosebud turning toward the light. The rosebud is unconscious of the sunshine that governs it. That almost irresistible drawing is prayer only when we know that it is prayer."[190] By His act of creation, God gave all human beings the instinct to pray. But the Holy Spirit desires to help believers develop their basic instinct for prayer into a disciplined means of grace that enables them to be God's joyful and fruitful coworkers.

Prayer is so linked with the image of God in human beings—even the shattered image in sinful men and women—that these fallen creatures cannot help but pray. Profanity and blasphemy are perverted expressions of this basic instinct. When the

---

[189] Abraham Kuyper, *The Work of The Holy Spirit*, AMG Publications, Chattanooga, TN, 1998, p. 628.
[190] Ibid., p. 630.

human race fell into sin, the basic instinct for prayer was perverted. Sinful people used prayer for their own selfish ends—not for the glory of God. The writer of Proverbs observes, *"the plowing of the wicked, is sin."*[191] Is he talking about whether the furrow is straight or crooked, deep or shallow? No, the plowing of the wicked is sin, because his motive in tilling the soil is wrong—it is self-centered, not God-centered. The prayer of the wicked is also sin for the same reason.

The Holy Spirit desires to help believers develop their basic instinct for prayer into a disciplined means of grace that enables them to be God's joyful and fruitful coworkers.

No spiritually dead person is able to acceptably pray to God.[192] There can be no life without activity. "As the body is dead when it ceases to act, so the soul that goes not forth in its actions towards God, that lives as though there were no God, is spiritually dead."[193] Someone without new life from the Spirit is not able to pray acceptably to God because he or she is self-centered. The desire of the unregenerate person is, "My will be done in heaven as it is on earth!" Hosea tells us about the prayers of people like this. *"They do not cry out to me from their hearts but wail* (literally, howl) *upon their beds."*[194] What they call prayer, God calls the howl of an animal. The Lord regards this as no prayer at all! A prayerless person is thoroughly irreligious.

---

[191] Proverbs 21:4 KJV

[192] See Ephesians 2:1 and John 9:31.

[193] Charles Hodge, *Systematic Theology,* Presbyterian and Reformed Publishing Co., Phillipsburg, NJ, Vol. III, p. 69.

[194] Hosea 7:14 NIV

Well, to those who are alive in Christ, Paul urges, *"Exercise yourself toward godliness."*[195] The exercise he urges is to be of a spiritual nature. Like the first followers of Jesus, Timothy was a disciple, i.e., a disciplined one. Spiritual exercise requires the proper use of spiritual disciplines. Spiritual disciplines are "God-given activities believers are to use in the spirit-filled pursuit of godliness."[196]

Scripture exhorts, *"Be anxious for nothing, but in everything by prayer and supplication, with thanksgiving, let your requests be made known to God."*[197] As we have already seen, *everything* includes our ability to pray. To be as fruitful as possible in prayer, we must pray for our ability to pray. Your goal of studying this book should be that your prayer life will become more powerful than it has ever been. Forsyth reminds us that, "Prayer brings with it, as food does, a new sense of power and health. ... Prayer is the assimilation of a holy God's moral strength."[198]

Loving Obedience—the Key to Increased Power in Prayer

"And whatever we ask we receive from Him, because we keep His commandments and do those things that are pleasing in His sight. And this is His commandment: that we should believe on the name of His Son Jesus Christ and love one another, as He gave us commandment. Now he who keeps His commandments abides in Him,

---

[195] 1 Timothy 4:7

[196] Donald S. Whitney, *Spiritual Disciplines for the Christian Life*, NavPress, Colorado Springs, CO, 1991, p. 14.

[197] Philippians 4:6 NIV

[198] P. T. Forsyth, *The Soul of Prayer,* Eerdmans Publishing, Grand Rapids, MI, 1916. p. 12.

and He in him. And by this we know that He abides in us, by the Spirit whom He has given us."[199]

God makes it abundantly clear that He releases His power in response to the prayers of His obedient children. For believers, the sovereign God is both our loving Father and our Commander-in-Chief. He commands and is gracious. A strong, spiritually fit Christian warrior is one who is consistently and lovingly obedient to His Commander-in-Chief.

Because God is sovereign He desires, deserves, and demands our obedience. He takes no delight when we turn our backs on Him in disobedience. Nor does He take any pleasure in mere dutiful obedience that says, "I'll do what You command—if I have to." Jesus said, *"He who has My commandments and keeps them, it is he who loves Me. And he who loves Me will be loved by My Father, and I will love him and manifest Myself to him."*[200] Only loving obedience delights the heart of our Heavenly Father.

Picture a mountain reaching into the heavens. A carefully prepared path moves around and up the mountain to its very pinnacle. The only way to the peak is to follow this path. Many have tried to strike out on their own. Some have left the path on the upward side, wanting to go straight to the top in their own way. But the sheer sides are too treacherous. All who have tried this approach fell to their deaths. Others have moved off the path on the downward side only to find there was no stable footing. They too fell to their deaths.

Loving obedience is like the carefully prepared path. Legalistic people think they can get to God their own way.

---

[199] 1 John 3:22-24
[200] John 14:21

They set up systems of rules and regulations to which they demand dutiful obedience. Scripture declares that salvation is *"not of works,"*[201] so that no man can boast. Lawless people pay no attention to the path and each person does whatever he or she desires. They acknowledge no moral absolutes and do only what is right in their own eyes.[202] Lawful people are those who truly trust Christ as Savior and Lord. God writes His commands on their hearts and they seek with the Holy Spirit's help to respond in loving obedience. Their obedience does not save them; their obedience is an indication that God has saved them.[203]

Obedience does not save people; their obedience is an indication that God has saved them.

Loving obedience is a Spirit-enabled process, a growth cycle composed of seven components: God's command, love from God and for God, petition for help, obedience to His command, manifestation of Christ, thanks for God's goodness, and praise of God's greatness. By ourselves, we do not have the ability to obey *one* of God's commands. But, Paul explains that when God is reconciled to us through faith in Christ, the Holy Spirit pours the love of God into our hearts.[204] And John adds to this, *"We love Him because He first loved us."*[205] God's first love for us gives us *"a new heart"* and *"a new spirit."*[206] By means of this love, God produces the desire in believers to obey His commands.

---

[201] Ephesians 2:9

[202] Judges 21:25

[203] John 14:23 NIV

[204] See 2 Corinthians 5:18-20 and Romans 5:5.

[205] 1 John 4:19

[206] Ezekiel 36:26

Jesus reminds us, *"Without Me you can do nothing."*[207] God commands, *"Call upon Me in the day of trouble; I will deliver you, and you shall glorify Me."*[208] Anytime we encounter one of God's commands, it could be seen as a "day of trouble," since we are unable to obey apart from God's gracious help. But *"the Spirit of grace and supplication"*[209] enables us to petition, to "call"; and when we call for help, the Father "delivers" us by enabling us to obey the command.

The Holy Spirit of God, who pours God's love into our hearts, is also the *"Spirit of adoption,"* who enables believers *to "cry out, 'Abba, Father.'"*[210] He *"helps in our weaknesses. For we do not know what we should pray for as we ought, but the Spirit Himself makes intercession for us with groanings which cannot be uttered. Now He who searches the hearts knows what the mind of the Spirit is, because He makes intercession for the saints according to the will of God."*[211] Left to ourselves, our prayer would be dominated by human emotion. So, with Paul, we must pray with the Spirit, and with understanding,[212] and God will graciously move us to obey.

Every time believers lovingly obey God's commands, Christ promises to "manifest" Himself to them, to reward loving obedience with increased ability to know Him.[213] And when God delivers and rewards, believers are to "glorify" Him.

---

[207] John 15:5
[208] Psalm 50:15
[209] Zechariah 12:10
[210] Romans 8:15
[211] Romans 8:26-27
[212] See 1 Corinthians 14:15.
[213] See John 14:21.

The closer we draw to Christ, the more aware we become of God's grace, goodness, and greatness. This awareness should move us to prayers of thanksgiving. Paul urges, *"In everything give thanks; for this is the will of God in Christ Jesus for you."*[214] A thankful heart exclaims, "How good of God to give me this!"[215]

Martin Luther urges us to remember that, "The Lord is great and high, and therefore He wants great things to be sought from Him and is willing to bestow them so that His almighty power might be shown forth."[216] This awareness should move us to prayers of praise. The Psalmist exclaims, *"Praise the LORD, O my soul; all my inmost being, praise his holy name. Praise the LORD, O my soul, and forget not all his benefits."*[217] Praise says, "What must be the quality of the being whose far-off and momentary coruscations are like this!"[218] P. T. Forsyth notes that petitionary prayer "is purified by adoration, praise, and thanksgiving."[219]

When it is difficult to know how to make petitions, we must remember that the Holy Spirit is the One who inspired all Scripture and continues to makes it profitable *"for doctrine, for reproof, for correction, for instruction in righteousness."*[220] The primary way He helps believers know what to pray is by

---

[214] 1 Thessalonians 5:18

[215] C. S. Lewis expands on these themes. See *Letters to Malcolm: Chiefly on Prayer*, Harcourt, Brace and World, Inc., New York, NY, 1963, p 90.

[216] *Luther's Works*, Vol. 6, ed. J. Pelikan, Concordia, St. Louis, 1955, p. 159.

[217] Psalm 103:1-2 NIV

[218] C. S. Lewis expands on these themes. See *Letters to Malcolm: Chiefly on Prayer*, Harcourt, Brace and World, Inc., New York, NY, 1963, p. 91.

[219] P. T. Forsyth, *The Soul of Prayer,* Eerdmans Publishing, Grand Rapids, MI, 1916, p. 37.

[220] 2 Timothy 3:16

guiding us to specific Scripture. The best prayer is Scripture turned back to the Father, urging Him to fulfill His promises. Jesus told us, *"If you abide in Me, and My words abide in you, you will ask what you desire, and it shall be done for you."*[221] The Holy Spirit enables us to understand Scripture and turn it into proper prayer. Thus, prayer that is kingdom-focused will not be merely sentimental; it will be scriptural.

> **When it is difficult to know how to make petitions, we must remember that the Holy Spirit is the One who inspired all Scripture and helps believers know what to pray is by guiding us to specific Scripture. The best prayer is Scripture turned back to the Father, urging Him to fulfill His promises.**

These three facets of prayer (petition, thanks, and praise) are essential for the growth cycle to function as God desires. But to be honest, we all know we don't always respond as we should. He enables us to do His will; then sometimes, we take credit for it. Or we try to do God's work for Him, trying to obey commands in our own human strength and miserably fail. At these times, the Holy Spirit becomes the Spirit of conviction.[222] He makes us aware of our sinfulness and motivates us to prayers of confession;[223] and we agree with God that what He calls sin is in fact sin! When we sincerely confess, *"He is faithful and just to forgive us our sins and to cleanse us from all unrighteousness."*[224] And once again we are ready to start the growth cycle over, to receive new commands from the Lord.

---

221 John 15:7

222 See John 16:8-12.

223 See Psalm 32 and Psalm 38.

224 1 John 1:9

We are also exhorted by Scripture to intercede for others.[225] God's providence places us in families, friendships, associations, and neighborhoods. In each of these situations, there are people for whom the Spirit desires us to intercede. Thus we must execute the full range of biblical prayer (petition, thanks, praise, confession, and intercession) in the development of our Christian life. "In God's eyes the great object of prayer is the opening or restoring of free communion with Himself in a kingdom of Christ, a life communion which may even, amid our duty and service, become as unconscious as the beating of our heart."[226]

God's providence places us in families, friendships, associations, and neighborhoods. In each of these situations, there are people for whom the Spirit desires us to intercede.

Christians from all ages have reinforced the principle of growth through prayer. "Prayer is the soul's blood,"[227] according to George Herbert. Augustine says, "Ask, seek, insist; by asking and seeking you grow big enough to receive."[228] P. T. Forsyth declares, "It is truer to say that we live the Christian life in order to pray, than that we pray in order to live the Christian life."[229] John Bunyan even goes so far as to say, "If you are not a praying person, you are not a Christian."[230]

---

[225] See 1 Timothy 2:1-2.

[226] P. T. Forsyth, *The Soul of Prayer*, Eerdmans Publishing, Grand Rapids, MI, 1916, p. 17-18.

[227] George Herbert, *Praying with John Donne and George Herbert,* "Prayer", Triangle, SPCK, London, 1991, p. 94.

[228] Thomas A. Hand, *Augustine on Prayer,* Catholic Book Publishing Co., New Jersey, 1963, p. 35.

[229] P. T. Forsyth, *The Soul of Prayer,* Eerdmans Publishing, Grand Rapids, MI, 1916, p. 16.

[230] Quoted by Friedrich Heiler, *Prayer*, Oxford University Press, 1932, p. 119.

This is not the place to list *all* the commands of God, however, there are some commands concerning aspects of spiritual growth that should be mentioned. Consistent development of these five aspects is essential for any believer to *"grow in the grace and knowledge of our Lord and Savior Jesus Christ."*[231] The following five commands deal with Scripture, prayer, worship, fellowship and witness. Consistent, continuous loving obedience is needed in all five of these areas.

According to P. T. Forsyth, "It is truer to say that we live the Christian life in order to pray, than that we pray in order to live the Christian life.

"Let the word of Christ dwell in you richly in all wisdom, teaching and admonishing one another in psalms and hymns and spiritual songs, singing with grace in your hearts to the Lord."[232] *"Pray without ceasing."*[233] *"You shall worship the LORD your God, and Him only you shall serve."*[234] Do not forsake *"the assembling of ourselves together, as is the manner of some, but exhorting one another, and so much the more as you see the Day approaching."*[235] And, *"You shall be witnesses to Me in Jerusalem, and in all Judea and Samaria, and to the end of the earth."*[236]

---

[231] 2 Peter 3:18
[232] Colossians 3:16
[233] 1 Thessalonians 5:17
[234] Matthew 4:10
[235] Hebrews 10:25
[236] Acts 1:8

New commands should not threaten us or weigh us down. They are opportunities for Him to manifest Himself to us. Each time this cycle is repeated we are put in the position to receive more challenging commands and to grow more and more like Christ.

Whenever we are challenged with new commands, we should realize the process that will occur. Bringing our behavior in line with our beliefs requires us to move through four-stages. In the first stage, we are unconsciously incompetent—we don't know what we don't know. We are blissfully ignorant. Stage two begins when new truth first comes to us. At this point we become consciously incompetent—we now know truth that must be translated into behavior but we are not doing what we know. In stage three we are moved to being consciously competent—we know what we should do and we are trying to do it. We feel mechanical, maybe even artificial, at this point. And in stage four we become unconsciously competent—we do what we should without conscious thought. The growth cycle repeats itself until Christ's High Priestly prayer is answered and all believers are one in Him and the Father.[237]

The illustration on the next page shows the growth cycle which is implied in Matthew 6:10, 33; John 14:21 and Psalm 50:15. *"Seek first the kingdom of God,"*[238] through Spirit-enabled, prayerful, loving obedience, and you will increasingly grow in oneness with Christ.

---

[237] See John 17:21.
[238] Matthew 6:33

Growth Cycle

We begin with the assumption of a believer who is seeking first the kingdom of God by praying *"Thy kingdom come."*[239] Start at point A, representing the command of Christ coming to you. You love Him because the Holy Spirit has poured His love into your heart (pencil in a line from point A to point B). Out of a heart that is redeemed and energized by the Spirit of God, your response to the command of Christ is a petition for the ability to obey (draw a line from point B to point C). Your loving

---

[239] Matthew 6:10 KJV

obedience (sketch a line from point C to point D) is rewarded by Christ's manifesting Himself more to you (continue the line from point D to point E). As He reveals still more of Himself to you, you thank and praise Him (draw lines from Point E to point F, and on to point G). Then He gives new commands to which you respond with increasing Spirit-enabled, prayerful, loving obedience, and so on, and so on.

Let's illustrate how the growth works; consider Steve's experiences. God impressed on Steve that he must seek first the kingdom of God. Steve is reading his Bible one day when he sees the command (point A): *"Be anxious for nothing, but in everything by prayer and supplication, with thanksgiving, let your requests be made known to God; and the peace of God, which surpasses all understanding, will guard your hearts and minds through Christ Jesus."*[240] Steve realizes that kingdom-focused prayer has not been a very consistent part of his Christian life. Out of love (point B), Steve prays for the ability to obey this command (Point C). He believes he should set aside fifteen minutes every day for kingdom-focused prayer. After a few days of doing this (point D), he gains a greater sense of God's presence and God's concern for his daily affairs (point E). Steve notices that he has become less anxious as he has sensed that God hears his requests and acts. Steve thanks God for His help (point F) and praises God for being his gracious, loving, heavenly Father (point G).

Steve continues "seeking the kingdom of God." In his daily prayer time, the Lord draws his attention to another command he just read (point A): *"And whenever you stand praying, if you have anything against anyone, forgive him, that your*

---

[240] Philippians 4:6-7

Father in heaven may also forgive you your trespasses."[241] Steve remembers some heated words he had with his neighbor who constantly played loud music after midnight. Steve was angry and confronted his neighbor when it happened one too many times. Because Steve loves the Lord, he desires to do His will (point B) so he prays (point C). As Steve prays and meditates on this command and its implications in this situation, Steve realizes that to obey the Lord here means he must forgive his neighbor. When Steve finishes praying, he walks over to his neighbor's house. He seeks to mend the relationship, asking forgiveness for his outburst of anger (point D). He explains that their friendship is worth more to him than a couple of hours of sleep. Steve then invites his neighbor for a cup of coffee and the neighbor accepts the invitation. The tension is gone; the relationship is restored. After his neighbor leaves, Steve senses the presence of the Lord with him in a new and closer way (point E). He has obeyed the Lord and the Lord has disclosed Himself to Steve in a way that deepens their relationship. Steve thanks God for the conviction of the Spirit and guidance to heal the damaged relationship (point F). Steve praises God for His faithfulness to him (point G).

Through this ever-deepening process, we grow *"in the grace and knowledge of our Lord and Savior Jesus Christ."*[242] Here the word *knowledge* means intellectual understanding worked out in the personal experiences of everyday life. This grace-driven cycle is repeated over and over. And, as we respond in Spirit-enabled, prayerful, kingdom-focused, loving obedience to our Commander-in-Chief, we are made strong in the Lord and the power of His might. We become fruitful, courageous

---

[241] Mark 11:25
[242] 2 Peter 3:18

warriors, praying about everything, all the time, with kingdom focus.[243]

As we respond in Spirit-enabled, prayerful, kingdom-focused, loving obedience to our Commander-in-Chief, we are made strong in the Lord and the power of His might. We become fruitful, courageous warriors, praying about everything, all the time, with kingdom focus.

Three Deadly Foes

We must remember that as we *"grow in the grace and knowledge of our Lord and Savior Jesus Christ,"*[244] we will become ever-increasingly more important targets for the devil. He will not be our only challenger, however. Scripture describes three formidable foes. The oldest usage of this triplet division of the field of attack is to be found in *The Book of Common Prayer* in a prayer for an infant, "Grant that he may have power and strength to have victory, and to triumph, against the devil, the world, and the flesh."[245] Much has been written on how to deal with these foes. If we fail to comprehend the differences, we shall be like searchers running

---

[243] This process deals with loving obedience to God's commands. It is also a helpful way to claim God's promises. The Apostle Peter tells us that God has given us these promises so that through them we may *"be partakers of the divine nature, having escaped the corruption that is in the world through lust."* (2 Peter 1:4)

[244] 2 Peter 3:18

[245] Donald Grey Barnhouse, *The Invisible War, The Panorama of the Continuing Conflict Between Good and Evil*, Zondervan, Grand Rapids, MI, 1965, p. 172.

around on land looking for a submarine, or an airplane pilot chasing backwoods saboteurs.

The Devil

Satan thinks he is greater than God; his weakness is his over-estimating his power. He thinks he is self-sufficient; therefore, he is proud. He thinks he can rule in God's place and establish his own kingdom. He cries, "My will be done in heaven as it is in earth!" The devil and his demonic hordes are spiritual beings who never have to stop for food or rest. For thousands of years, they have been studying human nature. And, while they cannot actually read our thoughts, through our visible expressions they are able to know many of our deepest desires. The devil and his demons are powerful—much more powerful than human beings.

As Christians, our power is in understanding our human inadequacy and God's divine sufficiency. Believers can do nothing without Christ. This means we are totally dependent on Him; and this dependency should keep us humble. When we pray, *"Your kingdom come. Your will be done on earth as it is in heaven,"*[246] we submit to God's will for us and are willing for God to work through us to achieve His purpose for history. God is all-powerful. He cannot be defeated; and so when we are yielded to God, we cannot be defeated. Our strength is in recognizing our weakness, and then by kingdom-focused prayer, relying on the Lord for His strength. Jesus told us to pray, *"Deliver us from the evil one."*[247] When we pray thusly, God's honor is at stake and He will not allow it to be compromised.

---

[246] Matthew 6:10
[247] Matthew 6:13

To counter satanic temptations, Scripture commands, *"Put on the whole armor of God, that you may be able to stand against the wiles of the devil."*[248] *"Therefore submit to God. Resist the devil and he will flee from you. Draw near to God and He will draw near to you."*[249] *"Be sober, be vigilant; because your adversary the devil walks about like a roaring lion, seeking whom he may devour."*[250] To deal with the temptations of the devil we must stand, resist, be sober, be vigilant; in a word—we must fight. The best example of resisting the devil is Christ's temptation in the wilderness. In the power of the Spirit, He used Scripture to defeat the devil.

The World

The Bible speaks of the world in three ways: planet Earth,[251] the world of humans,[252] and the spirit of the age.[253] The world, as the believer's enemy, is considered not in its literal sense but its symbolic sense. *The Oxford English Dictionary* defines worldly affairs as "the aggregate of things earthly; the whole circle of earthly goods, endowments, riches, advantages, pleasures, etc., which, although hollow and frail and fleeting, stir desire, seduce from God, and are obstacles to the cause of Christ."[254] Satan is the prince of all this.[255] Thus, worldliness is not a list of external taboos—drinking, smoking, dancing, etc. Worldliness is an attitude of acceptance of the fallen world's way of defining life.

---

[248] Ephesians 6:11

[249] James 4:7-8

[250] 1 Peter 5:8

[251] See Psalm 24:1.

[252] See John 3:16.

[253] See 1 John 2:15,16.

[254] The Oxford English Dictionary, 2nd Edition, Oxford University Press, New York, 1989

[255] Ephesians 2:2

In every age, some Christians have withdrawn to monasteries. They confuse separation from sin with isolation from sinners. This is not God's way to defeat worldliness. We must say with Paul, *"God forbid that I should boast except in the cross of our Lord Jesus Christ, by whom the world has been crucified to me, and I to the world."*[256] There must be a definite turning away from conformity to the world. *"For whatever is born of God overcomes the world. And this is the victory that has overcome the world—our faith."*[257] Faith first expresses itself in prayer. As we continue in faith we shall be more and more conformed to the image of God's Son, and thus we learn the meaning of *"Do not be conformed to this world, but be transformed by the renewing of your mind, that you may prove what is that good and acceptable and perfect will of God."*[258] Only the cross of Christ embraced by faith is able to render us dead to the world. The watchword against the world is faith.

Worldliness is an attitude of acceptance of the fallen world's way of defining life.

The Flesh

Luther in his Preface to the Epistle to the Romans says, "Thou must not understand 'flesh,' therefore, as though that only were flesh which is connected with unchastity, but St. Paul uses 'flesh' as the whole man, body and soul, reason and all his faculties included, because all that is in him longs and strives after the flesh."[259] Paul uses this term, not to talk about our

---

[256] Galatians 6:14

[257] 1 John 5:4

[258] Romans 12:2

[259] Martin Luther, *Epistle to the Romans,* quoted by Donald Grey Barnhouse, *The Invisible War, The Panorama of the Continuing Conflict Between Good and Evil,* Zondervan, Grand Rapids, MI, 1965, p. 180.

bodily desires but about the habits, instincts and tendencies of mind as well as of body that we refrain from the time before we met Christ. *"But I see another law in my members, warring against the law of my mind, and bringing me into captivity to the law of sin which is in my members."*[260]

Scripture tells how to defeat the flesh. Paul urges, *"Flee also youthful lusts; but pursue righteousness, faith, love, peace with those who call on the Lord out of a pure heart."*[261] Peter pleads, *"Beloved, I beg you as sojourners and pilgrims, abstain from fleshly lusts which war against the soul."*[262] If we are to gain victory over the temptations of the flesh, we must flee and abstain. We cannot stay around this foe without succumbing to its allure.[263]

There is a dangerous interplay between these three foes. Ephesians 4:26-27, for instance, says uncontrolled anger can lead to sins of the flesh, which open the door for the devil in the personal life.[264] 1 Corinthians 7:5 also tells us that the door is opened for the devil through unfulfilled sex in marriage.[265]

---

[260] Roman 7:23

[261] 2 Timothy 2:22

[262] 1 Peter 2:11

[263] The best single volume to study on dealing with the flesh is John Owen, *Mortification of Sin,* Christian Focus Publication, Fearn, Scotland, 1996. J. I. Packer's introduction begins with this observation. "I owe more, I think, to John Owen than any other theologian, ancient or modern, and I am sure I owe more to his little book on mortification than to anything else he wrote."

[264] *"'Be angry, and do not sin': do not let the sun go down on your wrath, nor give place to the devil."* Ephesians 4:26-27

[265] *"Do not deprive one another except with consent for a time, that you may give yourselves to fasting and prayer; and come together again so that Satan does not tempt you because of your lack of self-control."* 1 Corinthians 7:5

Of the three enemies, the flesh is the most strategically important because the flesh is the enemy "within the gates". John Bunyan has written one of the best manuals on spiritual warfare. It is an analogy that he called *The Holy War*. Though it was first published in 1682, it is still relevant today. Bunyan's early experiences in the great Civil War had taught him many things about the military art; memorable and suggestive things that he afterward put to the most splendid use in the siege, the capture, and the subjugation of Mansoul.

The story of *The Holy War* goes like this: Once upon a time, there was a town called Mansoul in a place called Universe. King Shaddai built Mansoul for His Son, Prince Immanuel. High walls that reached to the heavens protected Mansoul from all her enemies. There were five gates: the eye-gate, the ear-gate, the nose-gate, the mouth-gate, and the feeling-gate. Entrance to Mansoul could only be gained through one of these gates, and the gates could only be opened from within.[266]

Bunyan is correct in picturing Mansoul as impregnable unless one of its five gates is opened from within. The flesh is the enemy within the gates; the world and the devil are outside the gates. The world and the devil cannot gain entrance unless the flesh opens the way. But when the battle is too much for us—when defeat seems inevitable—remember, the battle ultimately is the Lord's!

Three watchwords, then, are the banners of victory in the life of believers. We are to believe and not conform, we are to resist; and we are to abstain—in single words: faith, fight and

---

[266] See John Bunyan, *The Holy War, Made by King Shaddai upon Diabolus to regain the Metropolis of the World or, The Losing and Taking Again of the town of Mansoul,* with a biographical sketch of the author, introduction, and notes by Wilbur M. Smith. Moody Press, Chicago, IL, 1948.

flight. For Christians to win the battles of life they must know their enemies—the devil, the world, and the flesh—and they must wisely choose to be loyal, to fight and to flee.

> **Three watchwords, then, are the banners of victory in the life of believers. We are to believe and not conform, we are to resist; and we are to abstain—in single words: faith, fight and flight.**

Martin Luther, an Example

Fredrick Heiler declares, "After Jeremiah, Jesus, and Paul, the German reformer, Martin Luther, is indeed the most powerful among the eminent men who had a genius for prayer."[267]

Martin Luther was born in Eisleben. His parents were reputable but humble. When a close friend, who was walking close to Luther, was killed by a lightening strike, Luther left his study of law and entered the Augustinian monastery. He became a professor of theology in the University of Wittenberg.

Luther preferred the Holy Scriptures and sound reason, before any human authorities or opinions. Many applauded the courage and heroism of this new opposer, but almost no one anticipated his success. For it was not to be expected that this light-armed warrior could harm a Hercules, whom so many heroes had assailed in vain.

---

[267] Friedrich Heiler, *Prayer, A Study In the History and Psychology of Religion,* Oxford University Press, London, 1932, p. xiii.

Luther prayed four hours each day, not despite his busy life but only so he could accomplish his gigantic labors. To work without praying and without listening means only to grow and spread oneself upward, without striking roots and without creating an equivalent in the earth. A person who works this way is living "unnaturally."[268]

Luther prayed four hours each day, not despite his busy life but only so he could accomplish his gigantic labors.

In Luther's *Larger Catechism* he remarks, "We know that our defense lies in prayer alone. We are too weak to resist the devil and his vassals. Let us hold fast to the weapons of the Christian; they enable us to combat the devil. For what has carried off these great victories over the undertakings of our enemies which the devil has used to put us in subjection, if not the prayers of certain pious people who rose up as a rampart to protect us? Our enemies may mock at us. But we shall oppose both men and the devil if we maintain ourselves in prayer and if we persist in it. For we know that when a Christian prays in this way: 'Dear Father, Thy will be done,' God replies to him, 'Dear child, yes, it shall be done in spite of the devil and the whole world.'"[269]

Luther's clarion call was, *"The just shall live by faith."*[270] And faith, in Luther's judgment, is "prayer and nothing but prayer. He who does not pray or call upon God in his hour of need,

---

268 Helmut Thielicke, *The Waiting Father*, James Clarke & Co., London, 1939, p. 65.
269 Karl Barth, *Prayer According to the Catechism of the Reformation*, Westminster Press, Philadelphia, PA, 1952, p. 9.
270 Roman 1:17

assuredly does not think of Him as God, nor does he give Him the honor that is His due."[271]

In Luther's time, prayer was perverted by medieval mysticism and works-righteousness. His return to the biblical prophetic model of prayer provided power to proclaim the truth and purify the church.

Faith, in Luther's judgment, is "prayer and nothing but prayer. He who does not pray or call upon God in his hour of need, assuredly does not think of Him as God, nor does he give Him the honor that is His due."

One of Luther's oldest and best friends was his barber, Peter Beskendorf, known throughout the town as Peter, the master barber.[272] In his letter to Christopher Scheurl in 1517, Luther included special greetings from "Master Peter." Hence in 1535, Peter, had known Luther for eighteen years or more. The barber was also known and respected by the university professors and had been a "surgeon" to Prince Joachim of Anhalt.

We may imagine when Peter Beskendorf went about his trade that, in the fashion of barbers, he carried on many a conversation with Luther, who, swathed in lather, could not reply at the moment. One time the barber declared that he, Peter, was going to write a book. It would be a book to warn everyone against the power and cunning of the devil.

---

[271] Friedrich Heiler, *Prayer, A Study In the History and Psychology of Religion,* Oxford University Press, London, 1932, p. xiii.

[272] The balance of this introduction is drawn from Luther's *Works,* Vol. 45, Fortress Press, Philadelphia, PA, 1962, p. 189.

Thereupon Luther took a book of Peter's and wrote a verse from John 8 about the devil being a liar and murderer. To this he added forty lines of humorous verse, beginning:

> "No one will become that sharp
> That he can know the devil well;
> No, tarred he'll be with his own brush,
> And will not in peace be left
> Unless Christ is there behind him.

Luther appreciated that the barber was a serious and devout man and later, in response to a request for a simple way to pray that an ordinary man could use, Luther wrote a thirty-four-page book, which you have been using to deepen your prayer life. Luther dedicated his book to "a good friend...for Peter, the master" and outlined a method for personal devotions, which he used himself and recommended to anyone as a pattern for developing a personal discipline of devotions.

Luther's suggestions are based on the structure and content of the *Small Catechism*, which he regarded as one of his chief accomplishments as an author. *A Simple Way to Pray* reveals a lifelong use of the catechism, not as a textbook for doctrine, but as a daily resource for prayer.

Luther would take his Psalter and whisper to himself the memorized words of the catechism.

Straightforwardly and clearly Luther described his own method, a "simple way." He would take his Psalter to his room or, if there were church services that day, to the church and whisper to himself the memorized words of the catechism, elaborating each portion in a way to kindle a fire in his heart. Luther recommended a set time for personal devotions, early morning or at night, and warned Master Peter against postponing them for some more urgent business.

Luther spelled out his method in detail—first taking each petition of the Lord's Prayer and setting down a brief meditation, keyed to the text of the catechism and the current situation of the time (such as the Turks, emperor, papists, etc.) Above all, he said, a Christian must keep his mind on his prayer, as a barber must watch his razor, an illustration for Peter's benefit. For the other parts of the catechism, Luther suggested a fourfold way of meditating on each item—as instruction, as thanksgiving, as confession, and as petition. This he illustrates in detail for each commandment. In a later edition that year, Luther added a section on the Apostle's Creed, extending the method to that part of the catechism. Luther wrote the book early in 1535 and it was so popular that four editions were printed that year.

Of course, the reader is not supposed to repeat Luther's meditative prayers word for word, and if the Holy Spirit should kindle the heart, all method and scheme should be abandoned to listen to the "sermon of the Spirit."

Of course, the reader is not supposed to repeat Luther's meditative prayers word for word, and if the Holy Spirit should kindle the heart, all method and scheme should be abandoned to listen to the "sermon of the Spirit."

A study of Luther's life shows the significant role of spiritual disciplines in his life, such as solitude, silence, listening, meditation, journaling, praying and obeying. All seven should be included in a daily cycle throughout the believer's life. This book is designed to help you develop that daily cycle.

As you continue to do so, ask the Lord to show you how to properly use them for His glory. He will show you that your daily time of prayer will not be a legalistic burden but a grace-driven, faith-growing delight. I pray that these last ninety days have been all you expected and more ... and I pray that this is only the beginning of your daily discipline of kingdom-focused prayer. May you encourage others to do likewise!

The Lord will show you that your daily time of prayer will not be a legalistic burden, but a grace-driven, faith-growing delight.

•••••

Discussion Guide

Discussion Guide

This *Discussion Guide* has been prepared to help you plan how you will work through the material in this book, as well as how you will start to pray with kingdom focus for fifteen minutes daily. Before you begin reading the text, be sure to read the introductory material in this *Discussion Guide* (through the Fireteam Commitment on page 118), as it will answer many of the questions you may have, or will have! It also will explain how the additional text, *A Simple Way to Pray*, is to be used.

Each *Session* in the *Discussion Guide* provides instructions for materials to be completed prior to your monthly fireteam meeting.[273] For example, read and work through *Session One* before your team meets the first month. (Fireteams meet once a month, for three months; each meeting lasts two hours. It is assumed that you are familiar with the fireteam concept, and that you are studying this book using that format.)

Session instructions include, among other things, study questions to be read prior to reading the material in the text. They also include reading assignments, which will prepare you for discussion in your fireteam meetings. Approximately thirty pages of reading are assigned before each monthly meeting, or an average of one page per day. (To accomplish this task in five days each week, plan to read on the average of a page and a half each day.) Or perhaps you will want to take an hour once each week to accomplish this task. If you decide you

---

[273] See *The Kingdom Campaign* booklet, available free from Serve International, for more information on fireteams.

want to cover the material in one sitting, do so early in the month so you can reflect on it during your prayer times throughout the month.

Six Learning Activities

Over the next ninety days, six activities will train you in how to be better prepared as a kingdom intercessor:
- ➢ Praying will make you a focused person.
- ➢ Reading will make you an informed person.
- ➢ Writing will make you an cxact person.
- ➢ Meeting will make you a bonded person.
- ➢ Discussing will make you an insightful person.
- ➢ Doing will make you a growing person.

Let us expand upon each of these activities.

Praying Will Make You a Focused Person

Prayerful study focuses your mind on discovering God's will. At the beginning of each *Session*, you will find the following printed prayer:

Lord, teach me, and my teammates, to pray. Give us helpful insights and understanding from what we study today. Show us what we need to understand better. As You show us things we are eager to try, enable us to do them. As You show us things that we find hard to apply to our lives, help us to be honest about them. Lord, as we review the questions in the *Discussion Guide*, focus our minds and help us find and obey the truth in what we study.

Start your study right now by meditating on this prayer; make its thoughts yours, and then pray it. Plural pronouns are used so that, in your thinking, you develop a kingdom focus and include others. Write the names of your fireteam members, your family, your pastors and other church leaders, and a few church members and other Christians on the *Prayer List* provided on page 133. As you develop your *Prayer List*, especially for this first ninety days, don't make it so long that it becomes a burden.

When you study the assigned material, frequently pause and ask the Holy Spirit to give you understanding and discernment. Anytime you find your mind wandering, ask the Lord to refocus your thoughts. Ask Him for grace that enables you to do what He tells you. Pray for opportunities to share what you learn with others—doing so will cause you to grow in what you are learning.

Reading Will Make You an Informed Person

The writer of the book of Hebrews states, "W*ithout faith it is impossible to please Him, for he who comes to God must believe that He is, and that He is a rewarder of those who diligently seek Him.*"[274] What you receive from reading this book will, to a great degree, be determined by what you *expect* to receive. Read with expectant faith, and you will receive more of what God desires to give you. Before going any further, pause and complete this sentence in your mind: "From this book I expect to receive _____." Write your expectations on the *Prayer List* provided on page 133. When you finish reading the book, ask yourself if your expectations have been realized.

As a member of a fireteam, you agree to read selected material according to a specific schedule. Start each *Session* by rapidly reviewing the material in the *Discussion Guide* for that S*ession*. Then read the assigned portions of the book and write in your journal your answers to the Four Filter Questions found on page 110, as well as the answers to as many of the discussion questions as time permits.

---

[274] Hebrews 11:6

Three Guards: Your mind will be fast at work as you read. But before you own anything in your heart, it must pass through three guards that protect your heart. Each guard is an automatic reaction; you may be unaware of it, yet you experience it. The three guards are as follows:

The Guard of Understanding: You must understand something to respond properly.

The Ethical Guard: After you understand something, it is more likely that you will do it if you believe it is right. You cannot do what you believe to be wrong without violating your conscience. God's word is *always* right, but some of its teachings may be hard for you to apply. When you find a hard saying, don't just pass over it. Make a note of it. Pray that God will help you properly respond. Share your concern with your fireteam and ask them to pray for you and help you.

The Emotional Guard: If you understand something and believe it is right, but fear that doing it will hurt you more than help you, you will struggle with doing it—or may not even try to do it. At times you will need to weigh apparent present benefits against actual eternal benefits. Paul put it this way: *"I consider that our present sufferings are not worth comparing with the glory that will be revealed in us."*[275]

Four Filter Questions: Four questions will help you think through and respond to your three guards. Tuck these in your mind:

1. What helpful insights do I understand from this section? (understanding)
2. What do I want to understand better? (understanding)
3. What is God telling me to do that I'm not afraid to try? (emotional)

---

[275] Romans 8:18 NIV

4. What is God telling me that I find hard to apply to my life? (ethical or emotional)

You will be reminded to review these Four Filter Questions before you begin to read the text. The Bible tells us to search and we will find. Keeping these Four Filter Questions in mind will engage your mind to search for truth. At the end of your reading, react to your thoughts in light of these questions by writing your thinking in your journal.

As you read, it may be helpful to do the following:
1. Look for things that you understand and are eager to do. Place an asterisk (*) beside these.
2. Put a question mark (?) beside anything you do not understand.
3. Note anything that threatens you with an "X." Also indicate why it threatens you.

Anytime you try to be what the Lord desires, the devil makes sure at some point you feel threatened. Deal with things that frighten you. *"For God has not given us a spirit of fear, but of power and of love and of a sound mind."*[276] If fear is there, face it with a sound mind (self-discipline), pray for spiritual empowerment, and it will vanish.

Writing Will Make You an Exact Person

Life that is worth living is worth recording. It is impossible to overestimate the increased benefit you will gain from each assignment if you will write down your responses to the Four Filter Questions and, as time permits, your responses to the questions from the *Discussion Guide*. Obviously, the more you put into this study, the more you will receive from it. When you are in a fireteam, sharing these written thoughts will bless you and others in the team.

---

276 2 Timothy 1:7

All members of the fireteam keep a personal journal. Do not let the thought of writing your answers to the Four Filter Questions and the discussion questions in your journal overwhelm you. If you will try investing an average of fifteen minutes a day in going through the text, you can easily work through all the material in one month's time.

Here are some practical suggestions for journal keeping:
- Do whatever works for you.
- Make journaling as convenient as possible.
- Carry a notebook for thoughts that occur to you during the day. Some prefer small notebooks they can carry in their coat pocket or purse. Others prefer to use a larger notebook.
- If you write your journal in longhand, be sure to write enough to retain your full thought.
- If you are able to use a word processor and one is convenient for you, try it. But, if your access to it is limited, stick to old-fashioned handwriting.
- Don't worry about sentence structure, spelling, or penmanship. You will be the only one seeing your writing.
- Don't just copy words from the text. Express your thoughts in your own words.
- Throughout the *Discussion Guide*, you will see the questions, "Do you agree? Why?" It is important to think these questions through. Don't blindly accept the thoughts in the text.

Now, before going any further, stop, take your journal, and copy from your *Prayer List* (on page 133) your answer to this statement: "From this book I expect to receive _____."

The Fireteam Commitment form on page 118 is for you to sign (if you have not already done so) as a reminder of your responsibilities to God and to the other members of your fireteam. Copy your Fireteam Commitment into your journal.

Why? Before a man was crowned king over Israel, he was required to write the law of the covenant in his own hand. This reinforced his knowledge of his responsibilities under this covenant. This handwritten copy of the law was evidence that he willingly assumed the covenant's responsibilities.[277]

Make journal-keeping a life-long habit, and you will find new depth in your relationship with Jesus.

Meeting Will Make You a Bonded Person

If you are not involved in a fireteam, consider joining one. Doing so will provide encouragement, understanding and accountability to you, as well as to others in the group. Remember that you will receive most from this effort if you regularly discuss this material with other believers. This may be challenging, but it should not be overwhelming.

Fireteams meet for three two-hour monthly meetings at an agreed upon time and place. The meeting place should be free from unnecessary distractions. It should be a place where you can easily talk to each other and pray.

Fireteam members pray for each other daily. If one is absent from the team meeting, the leader should make contact to see that the team member stays current on the matters of the fireteam. As members grow closer to one another, they ask to be encouraged for more and more significant matters in their lives. Becoming a kingdom intercessor is serious business! The devil will attack the members of the fireteam in a variety of ways—you need each other's support.

---

[277] *"When he takes the throne of his kingdom, he is to write for himself on a scroll a copy of this law, taken from that of the priests, who are Levites. It is to be with him, and he is to read it all the days of his life so that he may learn to revere the LORD his God and follow carefully all the words of this law and these decrees."* Deuteronomy 17:18-19 NIV

Discussing Will Make You an Insightful Person

In the fireteam meeting, the members discuss their written responses. The discussion should take about one hour of your two-hour meeting. You will probably not have time to discuss all the questions provided in the *Discussion Guide* for each *Session*. Your fireteam leader will deal with specific questions, but most of the discussion time will be focused on responses to the Four Filter Questions. Be prepared to express your thinking in these small groups by reviewing your journal prior to the meeting, and, if necessary, consolidating your thoughts or choosing the three most significant issues you want to discuss. Important insights gained from the discussion should be noted in your journal.

Doing Will Make You a Growing Person

The Apostle James exhorts:
> *Do not merely listen to the word, and so deceive yourselves. Do what it says. Anyone who listens to the word but does not do what it says is like a man who looks at his face in a mirror and, after looking at himself, goes away and immediately forgets what he looks like. But the man who looks intently into the perfect law that gives freedom, and continues to do this, not forgetting what he has heard, but doing it—he will be blessed in what he does.*[278]

It is an old saying that, "Knowledge is power." The words of James make it clear that knowledge without proper action is NOT power; rather it brings judgment! Maturity can always be determined by how long it takes us to do what we know is the will of God. The more mature Christian obeys more quickly, the less mature Christian takes longer.

---

[278] James 1:22-25

Obedience is the supreme test of faith in God and reverence for Him. *"Samuel replied: 'Does the LORD delight in burnt offerings and sacrifices as much as in obeying the voice of the LORD? To obey is better than sacrifice, and to heed is better than the fat of rams.'"*[279]   No one can sustain a right relationship with the Lord without obedience. Every thought must be made captive to and obedient to Christ.[280] Nothing less than "wholehearted" obedience to the truth is acceptable to God.[281] Therefore, each team member seeks to do what he or she believes the Lord is directing. Specific action-steps should be shared with the group. Before the close of each meeting, time should be spent praying for one another. At the beginning of each session there should be a brief time of reporting on progress in these actions.

Insight will come to those who pray and read. Greater understanding will come to those who, in addition to prayer and reading, record their responses to the Four Filter Questions and the exercises in the *Discussion Guide* in a personal journal and then regularly meet to discuss this with other Christians. But, ultimate benefit will come only to those who add obedience to all these steps, and do God's will as He reveals it through this process.

The Discipline of Praying

In addition to studying the material in this book, it is important that you develop the habit of kingdom-focused prayer. In order to begin your discipline of daily prayer, plan to schedule fifteen minutes each day—ten in the morning and five in the evening. Divide your daily ten minutes in the morning as follows:

---

[279] 1 Samuel 15:22 NIV

[280] See 2 Corinthians 10:5.

[281] See Romans 6:17 NIV.

➢ For three minutes, prayerfully recite the Lord's Prayer, the Ten Commandments and the Apostle's Creed (found in the Appendices of this book). Recitation need not be aloud, but it should at least be whispered so that your ears can hear what you say.

➢ For three minutes, read a portion of *How One Should Pray*,[282] reflect, and write your reflections in your journal for your personal benefit.

➢ Spend four minutes praying about your response to this material.

When you complete the material in *How One Should Pray*, begin again, repeating this process for ninety days.

In the evening, spend your five minutes this way:

➢ Read the day's *Daily Discipline*[283].

➢ Using your *Prayer List,* pray the suggested prayer for yourself, your fireteam members, one member of your family, your pastor, one church leader, and one fellow church member or other Christian.

Repeat the *Daily Disciplines* each week for the duration of the ninety days, cycling through your *Prayer List* of people to pray for.

Think of your prayer times as appointments with Jesus ... and keep them! Don't leave prayer for spare minutes, but plan a set time, continually making the effort to establish this discipline. If you have not yet completed the Fireteam Commitment on page 118, please do so as a reminder of your responsibilities to God and the other members of your fireteam. Don't forget to also copy the form into your journal. (See the bottom of page 112.)

---

[282] You will find *How One Should Pray* on page 17 of the book, *A Simple Way to Pray.* In the next edition of *Improve Your Prayer Life*, that text, along with the text, *Daily Disciplines,* will be included within this book.

[283] You will find the *Daily Disciplines* on page 11 of the book, *A Simple Way to Pray.*

Again, I encourage you—and challenge you—to make the next ninety (90) days a period of extraordinary kingdom-focused prayer. Ask God to make you a person of prayer—a prayer warrior! Invite Him to teach you about prayer, to show you more than you've ever understood before. Solicit His help to enable you and those for whom you pray to exercise yourselves to godliness, by grace through faith in Him alone. Pursue your relationship with Him, seek His face, ask Him to make you eager to spend time in prayer. By the end of three months, daily kingdom-focused prayer will be an automatic part of your life.

May these next ninety days be a delight to you and Him!

•••••

Fireteam Commitment

I desire to become a person of prayer—biblical, proactive, kingdom-focused prayer. To this end, I covenant with the Lord and members of my fireteam to meet ____ times:

_____

_____

_____.

(insert scheduled dates and times)

God helping me, I will pray that my team members and I will become persons of prayer. I will read the selected material as scheduled. I will write my responses to the Four Filter Questions and as many of the discussion questions as time allows. I will meet with the other members of my team at

_____

(insert scheduled location)

to discuss this material and to learn to pray with a kingdom-focus.

Also, with God's help, I will seek to pray 15 minutes daily, interceding for those on my *Prayer List* (see page 133).

_____

Signature   Date

Session One

Before you begin to prepare for this session, pray:

> Lord, teach me, and my teammates, to pray. Give us helpful insights and understanding from what we study. Show us what we need to understand better. As You show us things we are eager to try, enable us to do them. As You show us things that we find hard to apply to our lives, help us be honest about them. Lord, as we review the questions in the *Discussion Guide*, focus our minds and help us find and obey the truth in what we study.

I. If you have not read the booklet, *The Kingdom Campaign*,[284] please do so before your next fireteam meeting. This booklet explains why this ministry is necessary and how to implement it.

II. Read *Before You Begin* starting on page 7 and the introductory remarks of this *Discussion Guide* (pages 107 through 118). As necessary, review the Six Learning Activities found beginning on page 108, and use them as you prepare for *Session One* with your fireteam. Review the questions below for each section <u>before</u> you read it. This will put your mind in "search mode" and enable you to get more from your reading.

III. Pray daily that the Lord of the harvest will bring to your mind the names of six persons who are candidates for the

---

[284] Available free from Serve International.

fireteam that you will form in approximately 90 days. You will share these six names with your fireteam at the next meeting.

IV. Write the following Scriptures on a card, carry it with you and read it aloud frequently. You will be asked to recite or read these verses in your fireteam meeting.

But the end of all things is at hand; therefore be serious and watchful in your prayers. (1 Peter 4:7)

Be anxious for nothing, but in everything by prayer and supplication, with thanksgiving, let your requests be made known to God; and the peace of God, which surpasses all understanding, will guard your hearts and minds through Christ Jesus. (Philippians 4:6-7)

V. Review the Four Filter Questions found on page 110. Read *We Cannot Know What Prayer is For Until* and *Life is War* (pages 11 through 31) and write in your journal the answers to the Four Filter Questions.

VI. Answer as many of the following questions as time allows.

We Cannot Know What Prayer is for Until...

1. "Only when the ministry of the word is united with prayer does God release the fullness of His gracious power." (See page 12.) What is your reaction to this statement?

2. George Barna says, "A church's faith can be determined by the condition of its prayer life." (See page 14.) Do you agree or disagree with this statement, and why?

3. On a scale of 1 (being "little") and 5 (being "total"), how would you evaluate the amount of prayer in your congregation for the preaching and teaching ministry in your church? Why did you give this rating?

4. On page 14, the statement is made that this book uses an approach to prayer, which is militant and sometimes even military. What do you think this means?

5. After completing the prayer survey, how well does your behavior match your belief?

Life is War

6. "God ordained governments to maintain order within nations. ...Governments maintain police to deal with lawbreakers within the nation, and they maintain military forces to protect their nation from enemies without." (See page 19.) How important is it to pray for our elected officials, our law enforcement officers, and our armed forces? And why?

7. "Wars bring out the worst and the best in people, but they never leave people the same as they were before the war." (See page 20.) Why would this be true? Give an example if you have been in combat or have known someone who has.

8. "It is possible to lose battles yet win the war, and it is also possible to win battles yet lose the war." (See page 21.) When you have encountered spiritual warfare in the past, have you ever felt like you were losing the war, when, in fact, you may have only been defeated in one certain battle? How does the reality of Christ's finished work on the cross affect your answer?

9. Of the six aspects of a military model we studied, which one is most difficult for you to comprehend? Why?

10. Have you ever been on a committee or in a work-group, which functioned like the circle of processionary caterpillars because there was a lack of leadership? (See page 23.) How is a leader important to a group's reaching it's objective?

11. God put together some interesting armies in the Old Testament (Gideon's 300, David against Goliath, trumpet players against Jericho). Describe what God's motives might have been for superseding Von Clausewitz' rule of "superiority of numbers" (found on page 24)?

12. "The decisive battle of the cosmic conflict between God and the devil was fought on Good Friday." The on-looking disciples scattered in fear, watching the Romans torture and kill their Rabbi and Lord. Why then, do we refer to that Friday as particularly "good"?

Session Two

Before you begin to prepare for this session, pray:

> Lord, teach me, and my teammates, to pray. Give us helpful insights and understanding from what we study. Show us what we need to understand better. As You show us things we are eager to try, enable us to do them. As You show us things that we find hard to apply to our lives, help us be honest about them. Lord, as we review the questions in the *Discussion Guide*, focus our minds and help us find and obey the truth in what we study.

I. Review the Six Learning Activities found beginning on page 108 and use them as you prepare for *Session Two* with your fireteam. Review the questions below for each section <u>before</u> you read it. This will put your mind in "search mode" and enable you to get more from your reading.

II. Write down the names of six potential fireteam candidates which the Lord has laid on your heart to begin your new fireteam in approximately 60 days:

_____

_____

_____

_____

_____

_____

Add these six names to the margin of your *Prayer List* on page 133. As soon as you have the list complete, ask the Father to pour out upon them the Spirit of grace and supplication. Also begin to ask the Lord of the harvest to call three of them to be your fireteam in the next stage.

III. Write the following Scriptures on a card, carry it with you and read it aloud frequently. You will be asked to recite or read this verse in your fireteam meeting.

But you, beloved, building yourselves up on your most holy faith, praying in the Holy Spirit (Jude 1:20)

Give ear to my words, O LORD, consider my meditation. Give heed to the voice of my cry, my King and my God, for to You I will pray. My voice You shall hear in the morning, O LORD; in the morning I will direct it to You, and I will look up. (Psalm 5:1-3)

IV. Review the Four Filter Questions found on page 110. Read *War in the Bible* (pages 33 through 67) and write in your journal the answers to the Four Filter Questions.

V. Answer as many of the following questions as time allows.

Holy War in the Old Testament

1. Describe the difference between military war and holy war.

2. On page 37, we see that Moses and Pharaoh had a power encounter. What was the source of each man's "power?" Why is this an important question to your study on prayer?

3. As a believer, reflect on your position as a child of God— created in His own image. Who is your Father? Who is your Brother? Who else is in your family (other brothers and sisters)? What difference does it make when Christians see themselves as soldiers in a vast army, which has been

organized into families and churches under the headship of Christ? Is this the way you see yourself? Why or why not?

4. How were the Old Testament leaders of Israel different from the military model of leadership we previously studied? (Compare page 39 with pages 23-24.)

5. If military intelligence is one of the most critical elements of military success, how is it that there are so few accounts of spying or reconnaissance activities in the holy wars of the Old Testament? Was there no military intelligence? If there was, describe it.

6. Why was it important that Israel's soldiers be skillful in the use and maintenance of their military weapons if God was going to win the battle for them anyway?

7. The model for holy war described by Longman and Reid suggested several aspects, which support the idea that "holy war was regarded as worship." Identify as many of the actions required of Israel as you can. (See page 44.) What is your reaction to this idea of "holy war as an act of worship?"

Spiritual Warfare in the New Testament

8. Describe the differences between holy war in the Old Testament and spiritual war in the New Testament. (See page 46.)

9. What percentage of Christians do you think "don't even know there is a spiritual war?" (See page 48.) What about in your local church? How important is it for Christians to know this fact? Why?

10. List several specific changes that you have experienced (or need to experience) in your personal paradigm shift from "civilian" to Christian soldier? (See page 49-53.)

11. "Do your prayers often sound more like "an intercom between the den and the kitchen to order refreshment" than a soldier under attack in a foxhole calling in "air support" and seeking "orders" from your Commander-in-Chief? (See page 52.) How so? Pray for your praying, that the Holy Spirit would instruct you to pray as a soldier in the midst of a holy war.

12. List several of the attributes of leaders in spiritual warfare (pages 53-55). Faith in God's ability to lead through imperfect people empowers leaders in spiritual warfare. Do you agree? Why or why not?

13. Does Alfred Plummer's observation, "If in [Jesus'] life there was not only room but need for prayer, much more must there be room and need in such lives as ours," motivate you to pray? (See page 64.) Why? Read and pray through Mark 1:35 and Matthew 14:23-24.

14. "The spiritual warfare in which we are engaged may seem less concrete and tangible than was Israel's holy war for Canaan, but it is no less real and urgent." (See page 67.) What are some spiritual battles you are engaged in right now?

Session Three

Before you begin to prepare for this session, pray:

> Lord, teach me, and my teammates, to pray. Give us helpful insights and understanding from what we study. Show us what we need to understand better. As You show us things we are eager to try, enable us to do them. As You show us things that we find hard to apply to our lives, help us be honest about them. Lord, as we review the questions in the *Discussion Guide*, focus our minds and help us find and obey the truth in what we study.

I. Review the Six Learning Activities found on page 108 and use them as you prepare for *Session Three* with your fireteam. Review the questions below for each section before you read it. This will put your mind in "search mode" and enable you to get more from your reading.

II. Write the following Scriptures on a card, carry it with you and read it aloud frequently. You will be asked to recite or read this verse in your fireteam meeting.

He will lift up a banner to the nations from afar, and will whistle to them from the end of the earth; surely they shall come with speed, swiftly. (Isaiah 5:26)

The LORD of hosts musters the army for battle. They come from a far country, from the end of heaven (Isaiah 13:4b-5a)

III. Schedule with your fireteam to spend a night in prayer with them for the recruiting of your new fireteams. Write the date, time and place you agree upon:

_____

Ask the Lord of the harvest to call three of the six people on your list of potential names to be your new fireteam in the next stage.

IV. Review the Four Filter Questions found on page 110. Read *Basic Training* (pages 69 through 103) and write in your journal the answers to the Four Filter Questions.

V. Answer as many of the following questions as time allows.

Lord, Teach Us to Pray

1. The Apostles said, *"We will give ourselves continually to prayer and to the ministry of the word."* (See page 70.) Does it surprise you that, under the inspiration of the Holy Spirit, prayer was mentioned before the ministry of the word? Do you think that this order is arbitrary? Describe the balance between prayer and the word in your life. How about in the life of your church?

2. "Prayer is both a divine gift and a human activity." (See page 70.) "To improve your prayer life, you must begin by asking God to help you pray as He desires you to pray." (See page 77.) How often do you pray this prayer for yourself? For your family? For your church?

Exercise Yourself Toward Godliness

3. "Profanity and blasphemy are perverted expressions of the basic instinct to pray." (See page 78.) Is there someone in your life who consistently "prays" in this way? Pray for

them, that they would come to understand *why* they talk this way, and come to an understanding of praying biblically.

4. Prayer as a human activity requires discipline. Donald Whitney's statement is that spiritual disciplines are "God-given activities believers are to use in the spirit-filled pursuit of godliness." (See page 80.) What role do you believe spiritual "laziness" plays in the lack of prayer among many Christians?

Loving Obedience—the Key to Increased Power in Prayer

5. "The best prayer is Scripture turned back to the Father, urging Him to fulfill His promises." (See page 85.) What are some scriptural promises from God that come to your mind now? Try praying them back to Him for the next few minutes.

6. John Bunyan says emphatically, "If you are not a praying person, you are not a Christian." (See page 87.) Do you agree? Why or why not?

7. Describe in your journal a situation when the Holy Spirit took you through the Christian growth cycle referred to on page 89. Try to explain what happened to you in each of the seven stages.

Three Deadly Foes

8. Paul instructed the Ephesian "soldiers," and us as well, to "suit up" for spiritual battle. (See Ephesians 6:11.) In what aspects of preparation for spiritual war are you weakest? How can you address this vulnerable condition?

9. On page 97, in reference to battling the devil, the world and
    the flesh, it says, "We are to believe and not conform, we
    are to resist; and we are to abstain—in single words: faith,
    fight and flight. For Christians to win the battles of life
    they must know their enemies—the devil, the world, and
    the flesh—and they must wisely choose to be loyal, to fight
    and to flee." Earlier on page 62 it says, "Though there are
    significant differences between the devil, the world, and the
    flesh, our chief weapon against them all is one-and-the-
    same—prayer." Describe how the super-weapon of prayer
    invokes God to empower us to employ these strategies?
    (Tip: Luke 11:2-5)

10. Which of the three enemies is currently providing you the
    greatest challenge in your life? In what specific ways?

Martin Luther, an Example

11. As you develop a minimum of 15 minutes per day in
    kingdom-focused prayer, does the fact that Luther prayed
    around four hours per day intimidate you? (See page 99.)
    If so, go directly to Galatians 6:4, then Philippians 3:12-14,
    then to prayer – for your praying.

12. Suppose your barber or hairstylist asked you for guidance
    in his or her prayer life. Write a brief description of your
    present habits of prayer.

13. Do you use a catechism as a daily resource for prayer?
    (See page 102.) Why or why not?

14. How do you use the book of Psalms in your prayers?

15. Do you "whisper" your prayers, pray aloud or merely think
    them? Why?

Appendices

Appendix One

My Prayer List

From this book I expect to receive

_____

_____

_____

Fireteam Members

1._____

2._____

3._____

Family Members

1._____

2._____

3._____

4._____

Pastors

1._____

2._____

Church Leaders

1._____

2._____

3._____

4._____

5._____

6._____

Church Members and Other Christians

1._____

2._____

3._____

4._____

5._____

6._____

Appendix Two

The Lord's Prayer

Matthew 6:9-13

Our Father in heaven, Hallowed be Your name.
Your kingdom come.
Your will be done on earth as it is in heaven.
Give us this day our daily bread.
And forgive us our debts, as we forgive our debtors.
And do not lead us into temptation,
But deliver us from the evil one.
For Yours is the kingdom and the power and the glory forever.
Amen.

Appendix Three

The Ten Commandments

Exodus 20:1-17

And God spoke all these words, saying: I am the LORD *your God, who brought you out of the land of Egypt, out of the house of bondage.*

I.   *You shall have no other gods before Me.*

II.   *You shall not make for yourself a carved image, or any likeness of anything that is in heaven above, or that is in the earth beneath, or that is in the water under the earth; you shall not bow down to them nor serve them. For I, the* LORD *your God, am a jealous God, visiting the iniquity of the fathers on the children to the third and fourth generations of those who hate Me, but showing mercy to thousands, to those who love Me and keep My commandments.*

III.   *You shall not take the name of the* LORD *your God in vain, for the* LORD *will not hold him guiltless who takes His name in vain.*

IV.   *Remember the Sabbath day, to keep it holy. Six days you shall labor and do all your work, but the seventh day is the Sabbath of the* LORD *your God. In it you shall do no work: you, nor your son, nor your daughter, nor your male servant, nor your female servant, nor your cattle, nor your stranger who is within your gates. For in six days the* LORD *made the heavens and the earth, the sea, and all*

> *that is in them, and rested the seventh day. Therefore the* LORD *blessed the Sabbath day and hallowed it.*

V. *Honor your father and your mother, that your days may be long upon the land which the* LORD *your God is giving you.*

VI. *You shall not murder.*

VII. *You shall not commit adultery.*

VIII. *You shall not steal.*

IX. *You shall not bear false witness against your neighbor.*

X. *You shall not covet your neighbor's house; you shall not covet your neighbor's wife, nor his male servant, nor his female servant, nor his ox, nor his donkey, nor anything that is your neighbor's.*

Suggestion: As a memory aid, when you use the Ten Commandments as an outline for prayer, you might find it helpful to use your fingers to note which commandment you are currently considering. Start with the thumb of your left hand for the first Commandment. Shift to the thumb on your right hand for the Sixth Commandment.

Appendix Four

The Apostle's Creed

I believe in God the Father Almighty, maker of Heaven and
earth;

And in Jesus Christ, his only son, our Lord;
who was conceived of the Holy Spirit, born of the virgin Mary,
suffered under Pontius Pilate, was crucified, dead and buried;
he descended into hell; the third day he rose again from the
dead;
he ascended into heaven, and sits on the right hand of
God the Father Almighty;
from thence he shall come to judge the quick and the dead.

I believe in the Holy Spirit,
the holy catholic Church*, the communion of saints;
the forgiveness of sins; the resurrection of the body;
and the life everlasting.
Amen.

* the universal Christian Church

Selected Bibliography

1. Barnhouse, Donald Grey, *The Invisible War, The Panorama of the Continuing Conflict Between Good and Evil*, Zondervan, Grand Rapids, MI, 1963.
2. Barna, George, *The Index of Leading Spiritual Indicators,* Thomas Nelson/Word, Nashville, TN, 1996.
3. Barth, Karl, *Prayer According to the Catechism of the Reformation*, Westminster Press, Philadelphia, PA, 1952.
4. Bunyan, John, *The Holy War, Made by King Shaddai upon Diabolus to regain the Metropolis of the World or, The Losing and Taking Again of the town of Mansoul,* with a biographical sketch of the author, introduction, and notes by Wilbur M. Smith. Moody Press, Chicago, IL, 1948.
5. Calvin, John, *Calvin's Commentary on the Psalms*, 5 Volumes, Eerdmans, Grand Rapids, MI, 1948.
6. Calvin, John, "Prayer, Which Is the Chief Exercise of Faith, and by Which We Daily Receive God's Benefits," *Institutes of the Christian Religion*, Volume 2, Book III, 20, pgs. 850-920.
7. Durant, Will and Ariel, *Story of Civilization: The Lessons of History,* Simon and Schuster, New York, NY, 1968.
8. Edersheim, Alfred, *The Life And Times Of Jesus The Messiah*, Hendrickson Publishers, Peabody, MA, 1992.
9. Evans, Tony, *The Battle Is the Lord's: Waging Victorious Spiritual Warfare,* Moody Press, Chicago, IL, 1998.
10. Forsyth, P. T., *The Soul of Prayer,* Eerdmans Publishing, Grand Rapids, MI, 1916.

11. Gurnall, William, *The Christian in Complete Armour*. With a Biographical Introduction by J. C. Ryle. Glasgow: Blackie and Son, 1864; reprint London: The Banner of Truth Trust, 1964.

12. Heiler, Friedrich, *Prayer, A Study In the History and Psychology of Religion,* Oxford University Press, London, 1932.

13. Jeremias, Joachim, *The Prayers of Jesus,* Studies in Biblical Theology, Second Series 6, London: SCM, 1967; Philadelphia: Fortress, 1979.

14. Johnstone, Patrick, *The Church is Bigger than You Think,* Christian Focus Publication, Fearn, Scotland, 1998.

15. Kuyper, Abraham, *The Work of the Holy Spirit,* AMG Publishers, Chattanooga, TN, 1998.

16. Lewis, C. S., *Letters to Malcolm: Chiefly on Prayer*, Harcourt, Brace and World, Inc., New York, NY, 1963.

17. Lewis, C. S., *The Screwtape Letters*, Simon and Schuster, New York, NY, 2000.

18. Lloyd-Jones, D. Martyn, *The Christian Warfare*: *An Exposition of Ephesians 6:10 to 13*, Banner of Truth Trust, Edinburgh, Scotland, 1976.

19. Lloyd-Jones, D. Martyn, *The Christian Soldier*: *An Exposition of Ephesians 6:10 to 20*, Banner of Truth Trust, Edinburgh, Scotland, 1977.

20. Lutzer, Erwin W., *The Serpent of Paradise, The Incredible Story of How Satan's Rebellion Serves God's Purposes,* Moody Press, Chicago, IL, 1996.

21. Minear, Paul, *Images of the Church In the New Testament,* Westminster Press, Philadelphia, 1960.

22. Owen, John, *Mortification of Sin*, Christian Focus Publication, Fearn, Scotland, 1996.

23. Piper, John, *Let the Nations Be Glad! The Supremacy of God in Missions,* Baker Books, Grand Rapids, MI, 1993.

24. von Rad, Gerhard, *Holy War in Ancient Israel,* 1958 reprint, Eerdmans Publishing, Grand Rapids, MI, 1991.

25. Reid, W. Stanford, *Trumpeter of God,* Charles Scribner's Sons, New York, 1974.
26. Rommen, Edward, Editor, *Spiritual Power and Missions: Raising the Issues*, Evangelical Missiological Society Series, Number 3, William Carey Library, Pasadena, CA, 1995.
27. Thieliche, Helmut, *The Trouble with the Church,* Harper and Row, New York, NY, 1965.
28. Thieliche, Helmut, *The Waiting Father*, James Clarke and Co., London, 1939.
29. US Marine Corps Staff, *Campaigning: The United States Marine Corps,* 1989.
30. US Marine Corps Staff, *Warfighting: The United States Marine Corps*, 1989.
31. White, John, *The Fight*, InterVarsity Press, Downers Grove, IL, 1976.
32. Whitney, Donald S., *Spiritual Disciplines for the Christian Life,* NavPress, Colorado Springs, CO, 1991.
33. Whyte, Alexander, *Bunyan Characters of the Holy War,* Oliphant, Anderson and Ferrier, London, 1902.
34. Wilson, Jim, *Principles of War, A Handbook on Strategic Evangelism,* Community Christian Ministries, Moscow, Idaho, Rev. Ed. 1980.
35. Wilson, Marvin R., *Our Father Abraham, Jewish Roots of the Christian Faith,* Eerdmans Publishing, Grand Rapids, MI, 1989.
36. Zacharias, Brian, *The Embattled Christian, William Gurnall and the Puritan View of Spiritual Warfare,* Banner of Truth, Edinburgh, Scotland, 1995.